Fervor to be Free

A tale of tussle between mind body and us

Partho Dhang

First published in India in 2019

ISBN : 978-93-88333-75-7

Invincible Publishers

Registered Address: 201A, SAS Tower, Sector 38,
Gurgaon-122003

Printed in India by Excel Printers Pvt. Ltd.

The author takes no guarantee regarding the accuracy of the content of this work. The views expressed here are personal and the advice or strategies put forth may not be suitable all the time. The use of the many citations, such as books, articles, research studies, organizations and websites, in this work does not mean the author endorses them.

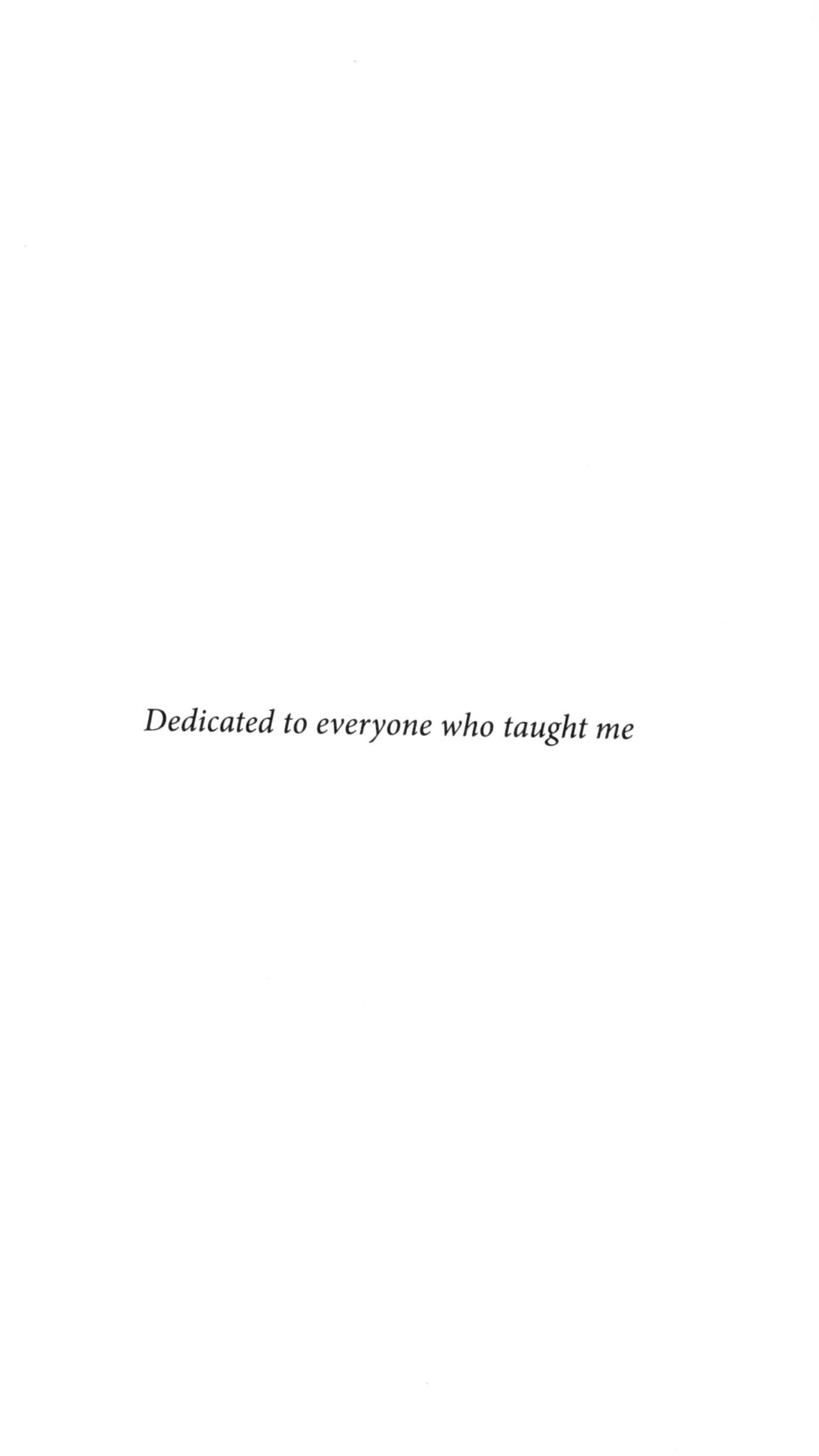

Dedicated to everyone who taught me

Preface

Writing this book was an effortless and yet intense experience. Events, thoughts, experiences, memories and all that I had read flowed into words. But a question, and challenge, was: Did I express them in the same sense I felt them? To get it right, I read the text sitting, standing, lying down, while travelling, between work, and at rest. I repeated it inside a cramped plane and in a luxurious balcony with a breathtaking view of nature. I read and re-read it countless times to ensure I wrote it rightest and to my truth.

My motivation to write all about myself was to share the mere experience of being human. As a zoologist I studied animals of all forms, but humans eluded me. I grew curious as I lived my life, caught between the animal and the cultural halves of being a human. We are bizarre beings; our thoughts are habitually unfounded and our actions have a way of their own. We do lot of thinking but our actions are often inappropriate. We hate other humans but end up copying them. We seem to invite chaos but lecture on organization. We look for competition but relish cooperation. We talk of privacy but post every activity online. We chase pleasure for happiness and seek happiness through pleasure. We are a bag of confusion. Then how did we become what we are?

Our living needs are of animal origin but we have elevated ourselves higher through the power of our mind. Mind is what made us human, a being, self-aware, conscious, intelligent. But we fail to explain why we are ready to jump to death to save another life. The body fears death but the mind chases death. Certainly, we have moved away from being animal. We have left survivorship and satiation and made purpose our singular quest. Purpose made us taskmasters and through it we found our true identity.

However, we also blame our mind for conflict, unease and misery. We try to smother thoughts and numb our feelings, intoxicating and poisoning ourselves to get away at the first opportunity. Little do we realize that with the aid of the mind and its never-ceasing thoughts, we have created a wonder-filled life around us and brought joy and happiness into our lives. With it, we have created God, constructed spiritual pathways, firmed cultures, invented tools, found cures, developed artificial intelligence, and realized consciousness.

This book is my journey through a world as I understood it best. A narration of me and my urge, constantly shifting between an inner spirit and outer demands, and finally hitting a finish line. This book is not my autobiography, nor a narrative shifting from step to stage, but a story. A story of incidents, experiences and thoughts which eventually yielded what I am. This is a story which helped me discover myself, and to the readers a reminder that they, too, have their own to tell.

I also acknowledge here the books which helped me shape my thoughts and actions, and eventually this story. Books by Desmond Morris, Eckhart Tolle, Osho, Ram Das (Richard Alpert), Pankaj Mishra, Rolf Dobelli, Joe Cormier, Sean Carroll, Yuval Noah Harari, and a few autobiographies and biographies had laid the basics. One book led to the other and I read writings by other authors. I have done my very best to quote them all wherever I have used them. In doing so, I might have missed out some, which I am sure has happened, but I believe that would be a honest mistake. As I catch the miss-outs in the days to come, they will all be included in the subsequent prints.

Partho Dhang

January, 2019

Content

1. Welcome to Life

A Restless State

The feeling of being miserable eats most of us. The lull after the high of a jolly-go-round trip, a sortie to the mall, or a get-together can be unsettling at times. Soon after, people jump to the next action to stay sane. Social media has become a preferred way to continue the euphoric mood. I often wonder: What would be the state of most of humanity without social media? It has triggered chatting, sharing, travel frenzy and countless copycat actions as pastime. The social media bustle has evolved as perhaps the greatest peacetime activity in recent times. It has surpassed meditation in the sincerity and intensity and drugs in its addictiveness. It seems to have helped calm the masses and keep them pre-occupied and content. Yet, it has not helped alleviate the misery inside.

I have felt that part of the reason for our misery is our dissociative relationship with the natural environment. We distanced ourselves from nature and from natural law. We live a life contradicting nature to a great extent. While nature dissipates, we are hardwired to accumulate. Nature lives in the present and we love our future. Nature creates for a purpose, while we do the same driven by profiteering. Our lives have changed from living in the open environment, to a form of caged living. As zoo animals, we have lost connectivity with the living world. I recall how years ago while driving out of the city on our first college trip, a city-reared classmate was amazed at the sight of vast stretches of rice fields alongside the rail track and had innocently remarked that it was a "beautiful golf course". Similarly, once when a good friend asked his son where the chicken came from, he got a spontaneous answer far from what he had expected: "Dad, from the supermarket of course." Immediately, my friend decided it was time to plan a trip to some rural location to help his growing son connect with nature and understand the process of growing food. I bet the boy would have needed it right away, before the supermarkets took over the last patch of the remaining land.

Our lives start with our birth on a metal bed in a concrete, air-conditioned room. Babyhood is spent in the crib, amidst the smell of lotions, sanitizers, plastic and foam, in a room filled with inanimate objects, fluffy toys, overwhelming colors, and excessive attention. Food comes from a tin can. And then, we are baptized, given a name under an invented ritual in a concrete building. We grow up following some faith that talks about an elusive creator for the whole of humankind. All the time, we are discreetly cautioned that this creator is one of a kind, checking and counting our sins, and that punishment looms somewhere. Natural urges of lust, greed, stealing, lying are red-flagged everywhere. However, quick remedies to cleanse are also made available. Most of one's adulthood is spent in manipulation and accumulation. Finally, forces in the body-mind start questioning the reasons for the entrapped and miserable feeling. To make peace, we engage in community service, creating awareness about love for nature, and volunteerism. Harmony is restored to some extent, but it is too late. Misery is written all over this human culture. Why blame the body?

While the tussle is played out inside, the human body is, however, a story of success. I would have been dead before age five if it hadn't been for the amazing resilience of my body. It was after an incident of a high fall while at play. I, along with a friend, was doing a feat. In the process, I fell and my head hit the cement floor hard and knocked me unconscious. I vaguely remember the inside of the green military ambulance that was taking me from home to the campus hospital. Such was the impact that part of my skull had turned soft as pulp. My mind went numb, paralyzed by the impact. The body went into emergency mode to help me recover and pull me back to my senses. The medical examination did not show major damage and I was discharged from hospital after a few hours. It took me some time to recover and come to proper consciousness. The second incident was after I had accidentally consumed contaminated water while on a trip. The body immediately went into overdrive, trying to purge the toxin. For the next few hours, I threw up froth and passed watery stool without a respite. Medical intervention came late but just in time for an evacuation. Complete recovery took a few weeks in this case.

Being alive is an amazing affair. The body, starting its journey from a single cell conceived by chance, transforms into a mass with billions of cells, all unified as one, and working in perfect cohesion in an amazing self-protecting system. It is this system that has sustained me and allowed me to grow and experience pleasures of the years of life that followed. The body acquired a character, likes and dislikes, and gave me an identity of my own. Years of experiences stored as memories helped me protect myself and not repeat past mistakes. The past thus holds significance to me: it prepared me for the future. Despite the writing on the wall that 'past is past, live in the present', I often visit the past for inspiration and reflection.

Life came a long way from those childhood experiences and turned me into a fifty-year-old. To celebrate those many years lived, I decided to gift myself a top-of-the-line sports utility vehicle. Loaded with power and up-to-date features for comfort, drive and safety, it was a treat I had suddenly decided to give myself without announcement or fanfare. Friends had coaxed me to go and get it, but it also made sense to me as my car was in dire need of troubleshooting. I had never been the 'celebration' type by nature, mainly out of a fear that the sensation of high would quickly pass leaving me in a miserable low.

I decided to take the machine for a long drive to experience the sensation it promised. I had chalked out a plan to take it around the northern loop of the country. We would drive it from Manila, following the western coastal road, and return along the eastern side, making a circle stretching over a 1000 kilometer. My driver and I would drive in shifts with a single night halt.

Soon we were passing through picturesque landscapes of the western coast. The road was flat with easy curves. There were mountain ranges to the right all the way in the first leg, and the glistening sea to the left. The road cut through the hillside, which was nearly a postcard setting. The sun piping through the adjoining tree lines made the view breathtaking. I was relaxed and enjoyed the warmth of the sun through the car windshield. It was not my shift on the wheel, so I was enjoying the sights, ruminating on random thoughts. I turned over and asked my driver casually, "What is the single most important thing you would want if you were given the chance to have it?" Without taking his eyes off the road, he said, "Money". I remember how spontaneously he had reacted to my casual inquiry. He then turned and with a mischievous smile said, "Can I add a girlfriend to the list?" I was not surprised at all by his remark, but hearing it first hand and spontaneously made it significant. He, in fact, answered a primordial need and essence of all living forms and bodies. His answer summed up the need of every living organism: comfort and a mate. But I wish he knew better. Today, I continue to seek something more. I am hungry for the next thing, a further betterment. It is an ever-present urge. I often ponder my restless state.

An Illusory Mind

I grew up idolizing others. That was how my surrounding world was, and I succumbed to the trend. School was where it originated. Top performers in studies and extracurricular activities were regularly rewarded, paraded, and projected as idols for others to emulate. I was challenged by these comparisons. They seemed to get the best treatment on the campus. In college, they were the ones who got the best jobs or immigrated to the West. However, few knew I was never content with such paltry competition and was looking much further. I started adoring sportsmen and adventurers at first. It later shifted to authors, innovators and creative people. Little did I realize then that I was idolizing mere actions and activities of these people, not the human in them. Achievements in the cricket field, some act of bravery, a great artistic composition, a best-selling book or ground-breaking invention attracted me, not the humans behind them. In fact, I barely knew the humans behind them at all. Why then idolize someone I do not know as a person? I saw many of these successful personas get into controversies, from street brawls, brash living to addiction and depression. Some were suffering and needed help and treatment. As I write this, the breaking news on CNN is of the famed TV personality Anthony Bourdain committing suicide in his hotel room. He was at work in France, doing another of his food shows. I have watched him on television, eating his way around the world and through many cultures. On television, his work seemed to be filled with fun and frolic. I liked his job and watched him often. Having achieved fame, he chose the path to end his life. It was a runaway mind killing a wonder-filled body. Ending the magnificence of life is too common among achievers. A famous fashion designer and brand leader, Kate Spade did the same weeks before Bourdain and the news was all over. I am sure investigators will dig up the causes. Yet, I believe nothing but their mind killed them. Mind does not register achievement and is never impressed by accolades. Somehow, the biochemistry of success seems not to last long in our body. It fades away as soon as the show ends. The mind goes back to looking for the next comparison and competition, taking us to the rudimentary core of human existence and behavior: survival of the fittest.

I had realized growing up that I had to push away idol copying and focus on meaningful living. I need to cultivate my mind. A good mind is the only way to a "good life". Eckhart Tolle's book, *A New Earth*, lucidly describes the nature of the human mind.[(1)] He says that "a mind from the start is close to be called dysfunctional", or simply mad. Religious scholars have understood it and have described it variously. Hindus called the mind as one which is in a state of "maya", or delusion. Buddhists say it is filled with "Dukha", or suffering, and Christians say it is in a state of "collective sin", meaning "missing the mark or target". Reading these suddenly made me feel the mind seemed an unreliable thing to carry around.

The mind is illusory. In *The Tears of My Soul*, the true story of a North Korean Spy, Kim Hyun Hee narrates how the nature of the mind can be changed through simple manipulation. The mind can be tricked. Thus, we fall prey to being brain-washed. On November 29, 1987, two North Koreans, involved in the terrorist bombing of a Korean Air Flight that killed 115, were arrested in Bahrain. One of them committed suicide on the spot. The other, the author of the above memoir, swallowed her poison pill, but survived. Extradited to Seoul, she confessed to the crime and was tried in the highest court. She was convicted and sentenced to death. However, the court later granted a full pardon, ruling that she was not the real culprit in the bombing but an innocent victim of North Korean indoctrination. She had been brainwashed into believing falsities as facts and had never realized she was being possessed. [(2)]

We live with our perceptions, which are often mistaken. We also live with our introspection, equally unreliable. It seems we venture into our life journey with an element of uncertainty. In fact, touring the world and reading about the past, I have witnessed the history of humanity: a bold depiction of numerous conquests, wars, genocides and violence. Our cultural history narrates practices involving deprivation, subjugation, banishment, extermination and deaths as means to our liberation. We started wars with imaginary enemies and ended them without any betterment for humankind. Wars resembled an evening game of soccer but with horrific outcomes. Ironically, all of the wars we have fought are a result of the human mindset and an illusion of the constant battle between good and evil. We continue to defend our past in the name of truth, justice and liberty, but deep inside we know we had chased a fictional idea and been fooled by our mind.

"The mind contains madness," as Eckhart put it.[(1)] The body fears being overwhelmed by a mind influenced by external forces and living defenseless. Astrologers, palmists, psychics, mind readers, religious heads and now politicians and product marketeers have mastered the art of influencing minds of unsuspecting people to their benefit. The greatest of all methods to control minds is the daily dose of advertisements. Advertising is a social phenomenon and plays tricks on our brain. They are intrusive and influence decision-making. They work on our emotions, stimulate our pleasure centers, test our code-cracking abilities, decipher the hidden signals and captivate us. Without realizing, they indoctrinate us. In the words of Peter Lunn, "TV ads make us more likely to buy what's advertised. Denial is not an option – there really is an elephant in the corner."[(3)] Sure enough, I see people around me who, influenced by advertisements, have changed to look and act like those billboard personalities. Their speeches are in tune with the advertorials. They buy advertised goods. They even make critical communal and living decisions based on social media advertisement. I see the coming of a new challenge from the circulating information and need to build an awareness to guard against all types of forces of calculative influences, to make the mind free for sound decision-making.

Trapped in Beliefs

Humans are brought into this world stocked with beliefs. No wonder humans are often difficult subjects to study. In my Zoology class, we left out humans from our course work because there was not enough time in the curriculum to deal with this complex creature. Added to this is the fact that we lack a true representative to base any conclusive inference on them. Such is their complexity that my class could have been easily divided in two halves, each on various attributes – between vegetarians and non-vegetarians, Hindus and non-Hindus, coffee drinkers and tea drinkers, Hindi and non-Hindi speaking, believers in arranged marriages and those against it, and countless such considerations. What defies us is not the animal part of it all but the culture and beliefs attached to it. Beliefs are dogmas, views and opinions, which one tends to gather, nurture and act upon throughout one's life. Beliefs are not something ancient, as it sounds, but more recent in the making. We continue to create new ones as we go along. How these acquired beliefs work in us can be seen in the cockpit culture of airline pilots. An airline co-pilot is not authorized to warn, overrule or take charge in the cockpit. There have been instances where their suggestions were dismissed by senior pilots, leading to fatal crashes. Florida Airlines and Asiana Airlines crashes in 1982 and 2013, respectively, show how dogmas can often be dumb. Investigating agencies concluded that the simple practice-turned-belief that a junior cannot correct a senior had led to these fatal consequences.[(4)] Beliefs jump truth, facts and reality and take shelter in us. This often defies explanation.

Sean Carroll, a theoretical physicist at California Institute of Technology, explains: "Humans are not nearly as coolly rational as we like to think we are. Having set up a comforting planet of belief, we become resistant to altering them and develop cognitive biases that prevent us from seeing the world with perfect clarity. But when we take new data, we try our best to squeeze it to fit with our preconception. This tendency is so strong that it leads to a backfire effect – show someone evidences that contradict what they believe, and they will usually come away holding their initial belief even more strongly."[5]

Sean Carroll gave a fascinating example, and I can recollect a few from my own life. His example comes from a study conducted by a researcher well known in the field of social psychology and later the same study was published as a case study. The researcher was studying an apocalyptic cult led by a woman named Dorothy Martin. Martin had convinced her followers that the Earth was going to be destroyed on December 21, 1954, and that "true believers" would be rescued by aliens the night before. The cult members were extremely serious. They quit their jobs, left their families, and huddled together to wait for the "big day". Nothing happened on that day. The researcher found that rather than pronouncing their leader's prophecy incorrect, the believers were more convinced of Martin's prophetic ability than ever before. They believed their small group prevented the Earth's destruction. They went overboard to spread their leader's prophecy. Bizarre human behavior indeed.

Beliefs conceived irrationally are like prejudices. As we grow up, we inherit a mind full of them and they influence our lives until the end. Beliefs shape our thoughts about people. It is the single most important thing we will encounter in our living lives – at school, university, work place and life. They exist as life companions. We constantly interact with people and their beliefs. Differences in beliefs trigger divide. People from other religions, ethnicity, caste, culture, class or country will be looked upon based on inculcated beliefs. Beliefs, such as those related to gender, will rule our judgment. They will determine how we treat a piece of information or how we execute a task. What preserves these deep-seated beliefs is the absence of complete rationality and lack of common knowledge, a common trait in humans, as theorized by Sean Carroll.[5] People gather information from different sources all the time, giving rise to differences in interpretation, an opportunity for biases. This includes people with trained minds.

Coming of Intelligence

Yet, restless humans with an illusory mind and firmly rooted in beliefs have created a wonder-filled world around. This is possible with intelligence. Humans possess intelligence. Intelligence lies beyond the mind and beliefs.[(6)] All that truly matters and are natural to humans – beauty, love, music, creativity, joy and inner peace – arise from beyond the mind and any type of laid-out belief, through the power of intelligence. Further intelligence has led to invention. Amidst the chaos around, both intelligence and inventions are working to make a pattern, a practical and workable system. My office chaos is taken care of by a handful of computers, and with them a system came to be in place. The clerks are gone. So are the ledgers. The answering machine handles the receptionist's job. Computers take care of countless computational work, data storage, paper-processing and task reminders. The computer even corrects an absent-minded staff and at times takes over the job of a missing employee. My product deliveries within the city are transported clear of traffic clogs by a fast-thinking software working in a route planner. This is the scenario elsewhere, too, and will soon be everywhere. It has been long realized that conflict in human judgment where it matters most in society must be removed to bring uniformity and organization, both of which are essential for running the systems in a fast-changing urbanized society. Intelligence is making this possible.

Soon, the entire human knowledge base will be held in computers. This singularity phenomenon as put forth by Ray Kurzweil predicts that "human life will be irreversibly transformed and humans will transcend the limitations of our biological bodies and brain."[(7)] Soon, a single body, a computer, will hold everything humans have ever known. This will be the most intelligent body ever to have existed on Earth and, amusingly, it would be a machine. When I realized the seriousness of this development, it led me to wonder: "Will this supernatural singularity be able to perform miracles, too? Will this be the new God I ponder?"

The process of computers taking over critical work such as decision-making and execution of precision jobs is now before us. Experiments for many more such replacements are on the horizon. Artificial intelligence, or machine intelligence, is taking over. In the process, the first to go will be tasks performed by humans. This intelligence will take the place of humans themselves. While robots perform manufacturing jobs at the workplace, a home robot will replace a human partner to give companionship. A company making dolls is already producing life-size human partners, which can outperform a human as a homely companion. It will greet you with compassion when you reach home after a day's work and walk up to you to take your coat off. Soon, we will witness people having relationships with such made-to-order robot companions. If we have accepted same-gender marriages, why not machine companionship?

A few years ago, I was nervous when for the first time I sat in a self-driving taxi in a business park. The concept of driverless taxis was in popular news, but experiencing it first-hand was quite a thrill. Though it was a short trip, I had doubts as to what the future was for it as a service tool. Much later, when my own car navigation application found a small alleyway after noticing a delay on the usual main route due to a blockage, artificial intelligence got down to work. I was more than impressed. It took me to the alleyway, but I had my doubts as it was not marked, looked private and was narrow. But I obeyed and in ten minutes, I was brought back to the main thoroughfare without a scratch. It couldn't have been possible with human maneuvering, but here the high-speed processor in my car did it all on its own.

Today, computers, or machine intelligence, run everything from space exploration, medical diagnostics, financial audits to communications, and more. Bank computers will soon decide an individual's eligibility and risk factors before processing a loan application. It will run the customer's profile through countless social networking sites, and check credit card usage, airline travel and hotel stay data to determine his economic identity. The judiciary, too, will be run by artificial intelligence. Machines will prosecute humans, and possibly send one to the gallows.

The power of processing has increased exponentially to a level where human lives are more influenced by sophisticated software inside high-speed computing devices, than by people's beliefs. The mind, too, is being controlled by machines, and machine intelligence. The new generation of millennials are growing up under the total control of an artificial entity. Every aspect of their lives is suddenly coordinated, irrespective of religion, culture, gender or race. As I observe, I find the new generation to be under some remote influence.

Human lives have become simplified, regimental but fearfully predictable now. I have a friend who looks after an online travel booking service, and once sitting with him in his office, I was informed about the algorithms working in his computer. He can now control the choices of his logged-in clients with great accuracy. He can stalk his client and even make him buy whatever he wants him to. It would be shocking to be in the shoes of such a client. This is possible because suddenly, our lives have become a choice between binaries – between "to have" and "not to have", "to want" and "to reject", "to like" and "not to like", "yes" and "no". The challenge of living is turning into the fulfillment of these simple actions, one linking to the next. This is all being powered by a hand-held smartphone, which is helping execute these actions. The device is not just a device any more but an aid – a part of the body, an organ. It has made humans, without them knowing, more intelligent, and probably freer. With a smartphone in hand, a human is a new being. The only need now is a good battery.

2. Nature, Nurture and Fate

We are Unfortunately our Genes

James Masterson, an internationally recognized psychiatrist, explained three factors which will eventually determine how our lives will turn out. It is something many of us may not agree with. But given deep thought, it turns out to be true. Our lives are eventually determined by our nature, nurture, and fate.[1] The genes we inherit, the surroundings we grow up in, and turn of fate have brought us to where we are now. While writing this book, I came across an interesting thought, expressed as "ovarian lottery", by Rolf Dobelli in the book *The Art of the Good Life*. He wrote: "Our place of birth greatly influences our success." He describes the phenomenon as "ovarian lottery". He said "the ovarian lottery doesn't end with your country of birth". Rather, he says, it has to do with the "area with a particular postcode and into a particular family. None of it is in your control and the values, behavior and principles given to you either help or hinder your entire life. You went to a school and into an educational system with teachers which you did not choose". Everything one does in life – from role-plays, decision-making, choosing a career, a city to live in, friends, contacts, to books and situations – seems like coincidences. He says, "What you are, you owe it to your genes and to the environment in which your genetic blueprint was realized. Your intelligence – being introverted or extroverted, open-minded or anxious, reliable or sloppy – is owed to your genes and the environment."[2] This realization makes me humble because a big part of me was determined by something which worked inside me beyond my control. This is indeed an ego buster.

My roots always held significance to me. It reminds me of the beginning – of this body, mind, and me. This, on the one hand, has helped me keep my bearings right but, on the other, held me up to my beliefs. Even though I have grown up, traveled, acquired skills and lived in different countries, deep inside I still carry my culture and beliefs – the same into which I was born. Today, I continue to live in the house where my father and my grandfather were born, and I have come to call it my home.

Our family belonged to a farming community from the state of Bengal in eastern India. The same Bengal which has its own Bay, called the Bay of Bengal, and a majestic animal, the Bengal Tiger. This is the Bengal where Amar Bose came from and resonated through the world with the Bose brand of must-have speakers. It is the origin of the world-famous Darjeeling tea, which grows in the northern part of the state. It has contributed three Nobel laureates to the world – in literature, economics and peace. It gave the world a saint who lived and worked her life there, and a Miss Universe.

Today, Bengal is counted as one of the poorest states in the country.[3] However, our family was better off than most. My grandfather, along with his siblings, owned vast tracts of rice fields across the state before the land reforms were made. Interconnected by rivers and canals, rice from the fields was ferried by boat to family-owned rice mills, where they were processed and later sold to merchants. Along with rice fields, there were farms of fish, milk, fruits and vegetables. The income was sufficient for him to send his six children to college. My mother happened to be the first woman in the area to go to a boarding college. For most of the year, she lived in the college hostel, visiting home only on breaks. The journey from home to her boarding took her on a riverine course, on a family-owned boat. Accompanied by a rower, a navigator who stood at the helm, and a family escort, she made many journeys between home and college. Every boat journey was timed to fit the river tide, to make the travel easier. Rain and shine comforters were on hand during each of these trips. She narrated her stories of the journeys many times to us at home. Recreating them in my mind, I felt the nostalgic moments of those bygone days she had lived through as a young woman.

Grandfather was self-made and lived a purposeful life until the end. He lived with conscience and with a heart. Known to all and respected by many, it was diabetes which hastened his end. I was there when he breathed his last. It was the first time I saw death. I was twelve and it was during my summer vacation in his home, in a village a hundred kilometers from Calcutta, later renamed Kolkata. Every year, I visited this place and each trip was fun-filled. But on this particular trip, grandfather took ill and he became bed-ridden. I vividly recall his last moments. With diabetics and multiple infections, his body looked frail and weak. The house filled up with people, while he lay with severe respiratory congestion. He struggled for every breath. Finally, he made a throaty gurgle, a sound I vividly remember and which only a man struggling from inside could produce. And then, the labored, noisy breathing stopped.

From a self-made successful man, he turned into nothing but a mass of flesh. The circle of existence had just played out in front of me. The rains came pouring and lasted for hours. A devout Hindu, he was cremated, his body consigned to flames amidst chants of Vedic mantras in the backdrop of the dark sky with sparkling, distant thunders. I stood there all along, soaking in the solemn surroundings until the ceremony ended. The Hindu way to bid goodbye to a lifeless body, a unique belief, and an ancient tradition. It reminded me of every moment of my being alive. Once the fire had consumed the body, it was left to die out by itself, leaving nothing of the living being it was but a handful of earthly elements.

My paternal grandfather was a school headmaster, a scholarly person, before he ventured into business. He changed cities and finally set up his metal trading shop in Bombay, now Mumbai. Teaching did not pay him much to take care of his extended family. My father, after finishing college, had joined him there as a help. Both were not business minded, so did not do well. At the first opportunity, my father moved away to join the Indian military services. Eventually, my grandfather's business folded up and he returned home to live a quiet life. He lived healthy and died of old age, as did my two articulate grandmothers. These were the immediate people from whom I inherited my genes and unknowingly imbibed beliefs and culture. Each time I visit home, I get transported to my childhood to be with them. Today, my life and my work could be a summation of all of these people. I see bits and pieces of everyone in me and it makes me think this is what I am composed of deep inside.

Unlike Charles Darwin, who was the son of wealthy society doctor and financier Robert Darwin and grandson of inventor, physiologist, philosopher and poet Erasmus Darwin, most of us are possibly locked into a set of genes, seriously limiting us from further improvement. We are unable to change our parents to enable us to change a part of our life and maybe a piece of our future just because our genes hold us to them. One born short can't choose to be a basketball player. It is the same with many others who aspire to become something but lack the needed shape, size or mental construct. In a class of thirty in school, we were distinctly different from each other in our tastes, likeness and abilities. The teacher struggled to impart common knowledge to all equally, but we remained divided till the end. Though we were all declared fit for the next stage, we grew differently. I struggled to understand why I failed to do as good as the others in studies, while I outdid them in arts and sports. We were wrongly taught we were all equal. In fact, we start unequal, and remain so for the rest of our lives.

Irrespective of this realization, we strive to be equal and work hard to reduce the differences. The booming business of body sculpture and look-enhancement is one part of this effort. It is turning humans into retrofitted ones to pretend to be a match, but it is not complete. Unique medical devices and implants, too, have altered our bodily limitations and helped us become equal. But these are transient again. This organic limitation, however, will soon be challenged. In his new book *Homo Deus*, Yuval Harari opens the possibility of a human creating "made-to-order humans". Making a baby of one's choice seems a possibility in the future. He writes: "Now, science might replace natural selection with intelligent design and might even start creating non-organic life forms with the help of genetic engineering. We will use direct brain-computer interfaces in order to create cyborgs – beings that combine organic parts with inorganic parts – and we may even succeed in creating completely inorganic beings"[(4)]. It is clear, genes will no longer limit us.

Nurture is where we draw Parity

Future babies, born or manufactured, will miss their childhood, which we were lucky to have in plenty. In fact, I have come to notice babies born in this century losing their childhood, the kind I had. My son's addiction to devices is unmatched. He outsmarts me in everything the device has, and so has all of his generation around him. This new breed seems to have found something in these machines. They are attracted not to the thrills and pleasures of experiences but by the machine's intelligence. He is learning not from actual experiences but from machine experiences. His imagination and skills are now locked up in sets of implanted programs. His tastes are now into exploring the virtual, not the actual. He is connecting the world through his head, not body. He reads the menu of restaurants and discount sales sitting at home. He seems to know what to expect during a trip even before the trip begins. I am confused and often ponder, "Is this a new way of nurturing? Will it eventually raise a new type of consciousness?"

I had a different type of childhood, though. I am proud to show off the scars of the cuts and brushes on my body, and countless other memorabilia. There are plenty of these memories. I cherish every event, often reliving them. That was a time I had felt my mind and body were in union, and the energy was the most palpable. The bicycle rides through bush trails, racing on abandoned airfields, hunting with the catapult, the thrilling game of cricket, loads of books of adventure, the train trips across the vast country, and lots more. These often come to me as flashes even now. I think each of these experiences contributed to making my personality and remains part of me to this today.

There are those who were born in my times but brush aside childhood as a stage of insignificance. It could be their failing memory, or perhaps those times were uneventful for them. As I read autobiographies of personalities, I have seen that only a fraction of the text is about their childhood. Instead, the focus is on events and achievements of the personalities in their later life – events from the external world which went into making the personalities, such as their actions and associations, when the fact is that half of what the personalities gained in life might have been hardwired within them at birth. We arrive in this world with a pre-programmed personality in our genes. This accounts for a great deal, or half, of the personality one acquires without one's choice. However, this half often remains anecdotal in script and scant in presence.

At birth, humans are more dependent on their parents than what is seen in any of the animals studied.[(5)] The fawn born as a prey is capable of outpacing a predator in a few hours after birth, while a lion cub knows to stay low and silent in the presence of intruders. Humans, on the other hand, are born developmentally premature with only one quarter of their brain developed, compared to three quarters in other primates. Each childhood experience goes a long way in shaping the structure of the brain – in turn, the thought process and, finally, the setting of the mind. Research has proved beyond doubt that identical twins originating from the same fertilized eggs are more similar in personality at the younger age, than in the later years of their lives. Studies have shown that 50-year-old twins have three times more dissimilarities, than three-year-olds [5], clearly providing some evidence that differences we experience as children at times get expressed in adulthood.

It is theorized that attributes of one's personality come straight from the environment – where and how one grows up. The likes and dislikes, fears and favorites and exposure and evasion get imprinted in the growing brain and, eventually, in the subconscious mind. It comes to control and influence our decisions and choices in later life. In their book, *Breaking Free*, authors Sheldon and Monika Kardener address questions such as "Why do our best intentions so often go awry? What prompts people to engage in behaviors that have the opposite outcome from what they wished for? What attracts us to our mates and then alienates us from them – only to find similar difficulties in subsequent relationships? How and why do we get in our own way of success?" Answers to all of these, as the authors suggest, are locked in our childhood.[5]

Children do not usually write their autobiographies in childhood. If they did, I wonder what they would write. I am sure they would skip subjects related to the senses, feelings, and everything of the mind. Childhood is one good time the body and mind have not separated and work in unison. Children remain adorable and lovable in this brief phase, where they are more in the body and less in the mind. I frantically search for evidence of childish expressions in text, written by children in their childhood. Instead, I found child biographies, and one of them is written on Charles Darwin by his father.[6] He writes: "He had been quite naughty as a young boy, and was definitely not considered to be as smart as his sister, Caroline! Darwin did not like school very much and found it boring, but he really loved nature and being outside. He enjoyed collecting plants and dead animals, and his family noticed that he liked going for walks on his own to find things that he could add to his collection." Amazingly, this does not sound different from the experiences of any other growing-up kid. How then did he become the great theorist we know him as today?

What we lacked in genes, we make up with training and by acquiring skills. A short player makes it into the basketball team through his dribbling and long-distance shooting skills. Double amputee Oscar Pistorius, born with fibular hemimelia, a congenital absence of the fibula in both legs, ran a sprint race wearing prosthetics, at the 2012 Olympics. Skill often prevails over our shortcomings and gives us an identity. Eventually, through it, we become what we want to, irrespective of our genetic limitations.

*

Growing up in India in the seventies was a bit similar to what Darwin would have experienced in his times. I grew up without television and telephone at home. Computers and internet were not yet dictionary words then. Travel was possible only by road and rail. It was the time India belonged to Indians. Every part of living was punctuated by tradition. East, west, north and south of the country were distinct in their own culture and flavor. The touch of Western ways was insignificant to the masses, and it was a time Indians were busy discovering their country. We did have spurts of Western culture hitting us at that time. What came was an antithesis of the West. I recall that in that period we had a phase of the liberated hippie culture hitting us. It brought hordes of young adults to the Himalayan foothills, seeking to break free. I had seen these backpackers at railway stations in their casual attires, slippers, sandals and backpacks, all over India. They seemed to be the liberated lot, unmindful of their surroundings and mixing well with the locals. For some reason, I have distinct memories of them to this day. Growing up, we as youngsters aped a part of the hyped culture, wearing bell-bottom pants and shoes with heels. In school, we were often pulled up to get us to have our hair cut to shape. It was indeed a muddle in the making, when the East strived to go West and the West was searching for the East.

Western ways were, however, distinct in all spheres during my growing-up days. I was raised in military camps across India. Even though we got our freedom from Western rule, the schools I went to, had Western style of teaching. The syllabus was tilted toward the West. We studied more about the world than ourselves. We were fed in on the advantages of the Western system, way of life, society, and their benevolence, understanding of humanity and underlying culture. I dressed like them in creased trousers and shirts, ankle-length socks, and wore shoes polished every day. I spoke their language. At home, we nearly lived their style. We always read the newspaper with morning tea, ate sitting at the dining table, slept under mosquito nets, all just as they did in the West. Doing anything differently was native. I can distinctly recall the best examples of this colonial culture that was exemplified by the famed Indian railways then. The British had invested heavily in building the rail system across India, and today it is one of the largest rail networks in the world. A few times a year, we traveled in the first-class cabin, a privilege extended by the Indian government to my father. The morning breakfast used to be served by well-uniformed staff carrying trays of sandwiches, omelets and tea in fine cutlery and clay teapots. They were polite, attentive, always knocked before coming in and said pleasantries before starting their daily routine.

Equally pronounced were the British ways on the military campuses. The military functioned as it did in the British royal military days. I grew up surrounded by the colonial style of life and among officers and men. Our homes were made in British style. Some homes were complete with fire places, chimneys, a front portico and a large garden. The campus looked like what it was in the bygone days, full of uniformed staff. Refurbished trucks and jeeps filled the campus with their characteristic diesel engine sounds. The sky was often noisy with pre- and post-World War planes and helicopters making routine sorties to an outpost, or performing drills. It felt like there was a sense of purpose all around.

Today, I see a typical culture inside me. I have come to love the distinct, purposeful Western lifestyle. I have never lived in the West long enough but have come to clearly distinguish between the life of a Westerner and an Easterner. People say the West is material-dependent and the East looks for everything in the inner self. I agree both look at life very differently from the start. I have stepped into meetings where the two cultures were present and have felt the distinction at the table. Although these differences between cultures are dissolving now, they are still obvious in the way one lives one's life and carries a profession. Western people often lead the deliberations by coming to the point straightaway and get to the result faster. Westerners express themselves clearly and keep emotion out of business. I have come to mix both cultures in me, as I love to live a life filled with tasks, take initiative, express my likes and dislikes clearly, match thoughts with action, appreciate hard-earned wealth and, at the same time, look deep within myself as the only way to real joy.

*

A part of my childhood that I could not dissociate with was the English passion for reading and cricket. I read all their top writers. It was my favorite pastime. Rudyard Kipling, Charles Dickens and later Agatha Christie and Arthur Conan Doyle. There were other Western writers as well who filled my time and imagination. But it was the game of cricket which I could not miss out on. Today, I remain an ardent follower of the game, an English invention, which India took pride in playing. A great social leveler, it evoked nationalism, passion, grit and determination among players and fans. We listened to running commentaries over a single-band radio whenever the country played. I cherish the memories of the midnight broadcasts when we played England, or the West Indies. The next morning, the exploits of the match were read and feverishly discussed while poring over the newspaper. Pictures were few and we had to stretch our imagination to visualize the match proceedings.

The country is obsessed with this game and I never lost an opportunity to play it. I played in all situations – big and small grounds, with full and half the number of players, indoors and outdoors, with different types of balls and with adaptable rules. But the best was road cricket. We played on less used or abandoned roads, or on the tarmac of an abandoned airport. We used tennis balls, light bats and no protective gear. The first two were easily and quickly arranged and, therefore, were popular. Another version was 'French cricket', played with a rubber or table-tennis ball. The batsman would stand with both legs together inside a circle and the bowler would try to hit his leg to get him out. The batsman hit the incoming throw for 'runs'. Runs were counted with the batsman swinging the bat around himself from one hand to the other in a circular motion. He had to count the runs aloud for the fielders to keep track of the total. This was an individual version of the team game and it required an amazing amount of dexterity to succeed. I played it well and was proud of my skill. I had cut-outs from magazine photos of cricketers all over my room and also drew them in picture books. Cricket had become a religion.

Attached to the game is an incident which also remains with me. It was just another evening in the park and I had played with all my energy. I was eight years old and my mates were also around my age. We were joined by an older boy, or, rather, a young man. He never played but had volunteered to be our umpire. We never complained, as we needed one badly to settle our on-field disagreements and constant brawls. That day, after the game, most of us sat on the grass and chatted for a while. Soon, it was almost dark and we decided to disband and retreat to our homes. I walked home with my bat. My house was the last one on one of the roads. While passing by a house, I saw from the corner of my eye someone inside the compound of one of the houses. He was our umpire friend. It was not his house and he was not from this place. He was bent down and working on the door lock, at least that was how it appeared to me at that moment. I stopped. The sound of my footsteps had made him straighten up and notice me standing at the gate. He came over and simply inquired where the neighbors were. He said he wanted to see them. I knew the neighbors well and was aware they attended regular prayer groups on specific days. I said what I knew, bid him goodbye and walked off toward my house.

The next morning, the whole neighborhood woke up to find the same house broken into and valuables missing. It was the same house where I had seen our older friend the previous evening. I was the only evidence and eye-witness. I was called to the crime scene and questioned. I saw the police team take fingerprints and a sniffer dog at work. It was like from the detective stories. The military police took me away to the station to gather information. The next few weeks and months, for the police I remained the only source of information on the incident. I was taken to countless missions to spot and identify the suspect. While I was at school, I still remember a couple of policemen walking into my class and requesting the teacher to let me go with them. It was exciting as after every new development I returned and narrated the motorcycle chases and trips to prisons to catch the suspect to my mates. The thrills from this one experience would remain a lifetime memory. The frame-by-frame recollection was as if from the pages of a detective novel. There was a time I even contemplated changing my life goal from wanting to be a cricketer, to a sleuth.

Between the cricketing moments, I had to also spend considerable time at school. Schooling plays a big part in the nurturing process. Look at the website of any school and one can see promises of nurture of every kind. It ensures a makeover with umpteen possibilities, and eventually a promise of success. The school I went to, however, did not make that many offers for a student, but it eventually taught me one thing – how different I was from the rest. I did not like it then as I felt left out, but today I consider it as a welcome strength. The 'being different' did me good. I could choose my way. But, earning good grades remained the singular objective then. The neighborhood I lived in treated someone by his academic achievements, laurels earned at school. This made school serious business. The captive environment of school had made me uneasy. I was the type who disliked the very idea of being tested. The pressure was undoubtedly relentless and I waited for holidays in any form. Ironically, later I discovered that we have had more creative contribution to this world from people who either dropped out of school or disliked it. Greats like Albert Einstein, Mark Twain, Oscar Wilde, Chuang Tzu, Thomas Edison, Bertrand Russell, among others, have tales to tell about compulsory schooling and their dislike for it. It is, however, a quote from Plato which made the most sense to me: "Knowledge that is acquired under compulsion obtains no hold on the mind."(7)

I had felt the same and asked why formal education came compartmentalized, unlike nature. I liked science but failed to connect between Physics, Chemistry and Biology. In the Physics class I failed to understand why water had to be liquid, in Chemistry why it was H_2O, and in Biology why a fluid to quench thirst. We go on to become physicists, chemists and biologists, while water flows with its singular consciousness. I took this confusion as a challenge and somehow made it through my school years. Eventually, the school system rated me an average student and pushed me out but, thankfully, with a record of good conduct.

Fate takes us to where we are

Agree or not, fate plays a big role in life. Think of having great genes and being privileged while growing up, but getting crippled in an accident later. After leaving Cambridge, Charles Darwin received a letter telling him that a captain named Robert Fitzroy was looking for a man to go on a voyage with him, as an unpaid naturalist. Darwin's dad did not want him to go on and told him that he would consider it only if Darwin could find another man who thought it was a good idea for him to go.[8] It was a twist of fate that Darwin's uncle supported him and he was soon aboard the HMS Beagle, and later to make history.

The world around exists as we see it because of chance. It is fate which has brought us where we are. Accidents can permanently change the course of one's life in a wink. One such incident is still fresh in my memory. It was a near-death experience and it left certain imprints in me. After my summer holidays, I was traveling along with my parents to our home town. It was an annual ritual and the only time we found for such a visit. It was the start of the long Indian summer. As a six-year-old, train journeys were much awaited and I vividly remember the fun while traveling. We traveled in style in the first-class train compartment, in a spacious and closed cabin good for four. Every journey lasted anything from 30 to 36 hours, crisscrossing the vast expanse of the Indian plains. The train made halts at stations in big cities and small towns.

At one such station along the way, we decided to fill our drinking water bottles. Bottled drinking water was not in the market then. Fetching water from public drinking-water taps at train stations was usually a tense affair. When the train pulls up at a station, one must get down and rush to the nearest drinking water point, stand in a mini queue often, fill the bottle, and hurry back. All this should be done precisely, or one risked missing the train. And a missed train was nearly a whole missed trip in those days. We had handed our bottles to a fellow passenger to fill as he went out to stretch his legs. He brought the water bottle filled as the train started moving. But the next few hours turned out to be a nightmare. The water was contaminated and drinking it poisoned me and my father. I cannot recollect much, but I remember the events as narrated by my mother. We were knocked unconscious with bouts of repeated vomiting. No doctor was on board. The only hope was for the train to reach the next station. The train staff were at hand to help as hours passed. Finally, we were evacuated in the city of Nagpur, a district headquarters in Maharashtra state, and provided emergency medical attention in the railway waiting room. For the next few hours, I slipped in and out of consciousness. I can recall some of those moments and it surprises me how it stuck with me for so long. We stayed a few hours in the rehabilitation area of the station before being declared somewhat fit to travel to our destination. For a few weeks, I slept day and night in a state of semi-coma, recovering from the accident. It was an incident I was too young to bring to experience, but it is one I won't forget.

*

I probed fate deeper. In fact, the many discoveries and inventions, the fruits of which we use and enjoy, involved serendipity in some way. The list is long. How gelatin, most drugs, x-ray, sweeteners, glue and millions of items came to us is a matter of twist of fate. Each of these has vastly improved human life to a level where our lives would be unthinkable without them. But another turn of fate was responsible for something greater than all of these material inventions. It was the discovery of how humanity thinks and takes refuge today – the birth of consciousness. Pankaj Mishra wrote in his book *End of Suffering*: "The Buddha was most likely not a prince, but a member of a republican oligarchy. Prince or not, he was a sheltered youth and his naivety in worldly matters probably gave him a peculiar advantage of noticing suffering as if no one had noticed it before him, which also helped him to discover in suffering a fundamental truth of the human condition and made him dwell at length upon its cause and cure." Sitting under a *jambu* tree, Buddha saw the cycle of life unfold before him, from laboring men and animals, to affairs of running the state. He saw suffering somewhere, by chance, and pinned it as a cause of human impairment. A chance meeting with a wandering monk and sighting of an old, sick and dead man might have eventually made Buddha decide to move away from a household to homelessness.[9] His moment of realization was not an act of desire. Rather, it was born out of a feeling which rested deep inside him and came from his environment, and which his fate brought him to witness.

Fate took another turn for me. It was an event which allowed me to get a grip on my life again. From the closed and protective corridors of school, I was freshly out in the open, unaware of my new surroundings, and unprepared. All this happened while I was living in the suburbs of Calcutta. The state was then under a pseudo-communist regime, democratically elected but using questionable methods. Their rule painted a bleak picture across the city. To remain in power, the hardliners in the ruling communist party had secretly churned the worker class into action, creating worker unions in all spheres of work. A class war against the rich, owners and educated had been unleashed, reminiscent of Mao Zedong's principles which culminated in his assuming power in China in the late 1940s. The rulers in Calcutta got the desired number of voters on their side to enjoy power, but the system and its unionist supporters disrupted the functioning of all workplaces. Labor unions grew powerful and, in a way, held the state to ransom. They kept heaping labor demands on running industries. Red flags with hammer and sickle signs and politically backed thugs influenced everything from street graffiti, posters, banners, culture, newspapers, workplaces, universities and even club memberships. Industries incorporated during British times and later turned into national icons moved out of the city, looking for greener pastures to escape the pandemonium.[10] New ones did not come to the city during this period, keeping the state away from industrialization and development. Today, the word 'gherao', a street word roughly meaning 'to surround and, effectively, to smother', is a creation of this city and the time. The term even crept into the Cambridge Essential English Dictionary as an Indian-English word describing "an occasion when people show that they disagree with something by standing around a person in authority and not letting them leave until they agree to do what people want".[11]

In school, I was away from the brewing political muddle but stood witness to the chaos around. I saw the tussle for education and jobs among the youth. I saw unemployment among my own kin and people I knew. It was a perilous situation with no fix in sight and it forced people with resources to move out to other parts of the country. I was too young to understand the politics behind most of it, but every adult I knew in my family and elsewhere spoke of it. It was a topic as common as discussing the weather. In the later years, however, the true nature of the tilt toward communism for the state dawned upon me. It started as a peasant movement in a place called Naxalbari, far north of Calcutta, with the movement's founder spewing fiery words such as: "only by waging class struggle – the battle of annihilation – the new man will be created – the new man will defy death and will be free from all self-interests."[(12)] Irksome words indeed, as I looked back at the state's history and my escape from the chaos.

It was by a stroke of luck that I had got an opportunity to migrate from the city right in the midst of the chaos. Our family moved to the city of Madras, a faraway land in those times. It was a breath of fresh air at a time I most needed it. Soon, I got admitted to university, a welcome life-changer. Instantly, I liked my newly acquired status. The most appealing was the indescribable nature of the freedom on the college campus. For the first time, I felt I was an individual, not foot soldiers, as it was in school. My classmates came from diverse economic and social backgrounds. For the first time, I saw the distinct and inevitable inequality expressed in the open. We expressed differing opinions and had a variety of plans and expectations from the world. We expressed differing desires and life goals. We discussed "good-life". For the first time in my life, I heard people talking of leaving India and going overseas for education, to make a living, or even for citizenship. Until then, I never knew this could be a possibility.

3. We are Product of our Times

Growing up as Generation X

I came across a Warren Buffet quote: "If I would have been born thousands of year ago, I would be some animal's lunch because I can't run very fast or climb trees."[(1)] My fate favored me most in this case; I was born in a time when I am no longer a piece of meat anymore, but a product of a generation which has changed the way the world lives and thinks today. In fact, it was during the eighties that I spent my youth. A National Geographic show had summarized in its series of episodes, titled 'The decade that made us', in which the eighties was called as "a decade characterized by losing authority of governments, a culture of freeness, redefinition of human values, and coming of technology. The influence of this period, particularly in politics, environmental concerns, gender movements, mechanization of work, and pop culture, can be experienced today".[(2)] The time had influenced me profoundly and today I am a proud product of the eighties.

In the eighties, India, too, shifted from a conservative outlook, where practically everything seemed to be scarce, regulated, or under control that prevented it from being liberal. The mood had changed, and it was upbeat. The country started the decade winning its first cricket World Cup. A mere game it may be, but it ran in the veins of the country as a part of its culture. Headlines had screamed: "India can do it". The generation, for the first time, felt self-confident as a world power and as a world beater. Soon after this, the country overwhelmingly elected a 40-year-old London-educated professional pilot as its prime minister, bringing youthfulness and modernity in governance. Information technology, powered by computers and data sharing and unknown in the country until then, took hold during his tenure. The period was rightly described by many as a period of resurgence for the country.(3)

Resurgence brought many ventures into the country. Items that we had never seen or used were suddenly all over the place. Personal computers came into use, replacing the old-fashioned ledgers. Motorcycles went into mass production, replacing bicycles. A Japanese mini car was rolling on the roads. Ownership of cars, unthinkable at the time, was now a possibility. Television came into homes and multiple channels beamed color pictures. Tele-serials with religion, history, family and youth as themes held us captive. Overseas television serials, too, were gaining ground, closely followed by MTV, with which came a generation of youthful exuberance. New universities opened up and started offering newer courses such as in computer science and biotechnology. India was modernizing. So were the people and their habits. With modernization, old ways were taken out of shelves and put into bins. A hint of consumerism was in the air for the first time. People spent money on goods, restaurants, cinema and travel. Belonging to this generation, which is now being put forth as a cohort called the Generation X or Gen X, was exhilarating.

I researched this group and was astounded to know so much work had gone into studying the characteristics of Gen X. I didn't believe there would exist a "generation type". Humans have been categorized by ethnicity, gender or geography but not by age group. Rich Cohen's description of this generation in his article convinced me in believing it.(4) He wrote: "A generation is the creation of shared experiences, the things that happened, the things they did and listened to and read and went through and, as important, and the things that did not happen." Gen X got a distinct culture into them and later came to be known as the "latchkey generation" due to reduced adult supervision as children, compared to previous generations, and increased maternal participation. Research shows them as active, happy, and achieving a work-life balance in their midlife. They have been credited with an entrepreneurial bent. To me, this is the generation which still has the memory of growing up in a computer-free world and, today, as rightly said, "they engage less with their online personas for selfie-centered promotion, and more to keep track of the world".[(5)]

I recall my own days growing up. What we did was unique to some extent. Our parents and teachers were born when India was a British colony. They had participated in the Independence struggle and nation-building. They knew how to live with scarce resources when the country struggled to grow food and provide basic healthcare and transportation services. They were nationalists, conservative and proud. They grew up with clear values, with a cultural conscience, and were ready to make sacrifices. They were mostly the first generation in their family to be full-time employees, a part of free India's first-generation workforce. We as Generation X were in a way the lucky lot. We had the right type of family, and attention from our parents. In most cases, we had our mothers at home as homemakers. Food was on the table, on time, and every time. Clothes were washed, ironed and ready to wear. Fathers had their significance in the family. They were pillars of security and support. We were independent India's first generation who had a chance to experiment, think more, and choose the best. Today, I am in the same cohort of Gen Xes, along with others who are busy altering human beliefs and culture. They are defining future humans. While Lary Page of Google and Jeff Bezos of Amazon are busy developing tools to decide how future humans will live, Elon Musk is prospecting interplanetary real estate opportunities.

Tumbling Belief and making of a Culture

The eighties saw the launch of the first personal computer by IBM. It was a crude device then, but, nonetheless, was the start of the human journey toward unraveling the mind. It was also the start of breakdown of a mainstream system which had held steady until then. The wandering hippies of the previous decades returned with plans to disrupt the system this time. In their first attempt, they were dismissed as gypsies and losers. Their attempt to find a way to break away from industrial-capitalism, which had come to dominate every aspect of life, was a silent rebellion. On the surface, the hippie movement may have appeared hedonistic, but at its core it was about creating new ways of living. This included creating their own tools and living methods that were not reliant on the mainstream system. The attempt was to bring liberation, freedom, new beliefs and an alternate culture.

Even though I grew up in a distant land, far away from the brewing culture, the change was in the air everywhere in the eighties. Suddenly, a part of California had found its way into a culture to counter whatever the world believed was right. There were many such social experiments around the world, but the one which influenced the rest of the world came out of San Francisco and, in particular, from a place called the Silicon Valley. Here, technology research, anti-war feeling, psychedelic drugs, free thought, community living, spirituality and intelligence all clashed in one place. (6) The result was a totally new culture, a belief system which remained nameless but distinctly practicable.

Out of this culture, one man named Steve Jobs ruled my thoughts above the rest. Steve was greatly influenced by the values and vision of the hippie counterculture. He came of age living in the epicenter of this social movement. He clearly embraced the hippies' practices and philosophies. Tributes to him highlighted his inclination to show how his business behavior was shaped by his distrust of authority and his willingness to expand his mind in many directions.

He travelled to India and followed an Indian religion to understand himself. His engagement with Eastern spirituality, especially Zen Buddhism, was not just some passing fancy or youthful dabbling. He embraced it with his typical intensity, and it became deeply ingrained in his personality. He was also deeply influenced by the emphasis that Buddhism places on intuition. "I began to realize that an intuitive understanding and consciousness was more significant than abstract thinking and intellectual logical analysis," he later said.(6)

The Hippies, in fact, provided us with a counterculture which, to a great extent, broke the shackles of mainstream thinking. An article by Stewart Brand in 1995, "We Owe it all to the Hippies", said it all.(7) The final product of this counterculture was development of computers, and computers came to symbolize a new way of thinking. Soon, a shift was underway. "Computing went from being dismissed as a tool of bureaucratic control to being embraced as a symbol of individual expression and liberation."(8) Then, there were those hippies who were heading for the countryside to live communally with a copy of the so-called Whole Earth Catalogue (WEC), a book with a wealth of information on topics from the best kerosene lamps to goat husbandry. This WEC is another cultural move that set us on the path of what we see and do today.(9) WEC was an American counterculture magazine and product catalog published by Stewart Brand several times a year between 1968 and 1972, and occasionally thereafter until 1998. The magazine featured essays and articles but was primarily focused on product reviews. The editorial focus was on self-sufficiency, ecology, alternative education, "do it yourself" (DIY), holism, and it featured the slogan "access to tools".(9) Finally, in the 1980s, the World Wide Web replaced the WEC, making every tool for living much handier, and breaking free possible.

Computers and computing power have changed us all. It changed me. By the end of the decade, I was sitting at a computer in my laboratory and processing my data faster than ever before. Pages and pages of numbers were analyzed in no time. The computer was now interpreting my data and inferring for me. New patterns emerged. New results were obtained. Newer thoughts were opened. I stared at it as an observer, while it computed for me. For the first time, I was witnessing the power of processing and computing. This was my first-hand experience of a nascent artificial intelligence at work.

Faster computational power changed how work was done in the country. It sped up our lives. It sped up everything around us. It was now possible to search, communicate, analyze, process and produce everything faster. Time as we knew it had vanished in one way but to reappear elsewhere in plenty. Hobbies, exploration and creative opportunities opened up. We were trying to cope with this new definition of time. Leisure came into our lives and we needed plans to engage in it. Earlier, between episodes of a popular soap, we had a week to ponder and discuss what would be next. In cricket matches, players stayed "not out" for days at the crease, just defending against the opponent's bowlers. Travelers slept in trains crossing the country. A reply to a letter was not expected before a month. Books were read from cover to cover to seek thrill and wisdom. But in the new culture, time got redefined and soon began to test our patience.

While it made time a trouble of some sort, it also exposed another fact – one needed to have money to experience and be part of this collective change. For the first time, I realized the value of money in life and developed the urge to earn it. I looked for economic freedom as a primary goal, more than all other. If I remember clearly, it was the first time I had such an urge. I also realized for the first time that individuals could live independent of the system and not be considered outlaws. Tools to live independently were suddenly available everywhere. I desperately wanted to be part of this new culture, and looming freedom.

Idea of Entrepreneurship

I travelled home a few times in a year from wherever I lived. This time, I had taken a longer break to spend time on a book I was editing. The good part about home is its tranquility – a farmland environment, comfortable weather, and plenty of fresh home-grown food. The setting is near idyllic, and I often get into meditative mode without even having to try to. I had done a fair bit of writing work here. This time, I was working on my fourth book in a series of books I had been invited to publish by a UK-based publisher and organization specializing in environment, agriculture, climate change and sustainable development.

I had used my time between my writing to contemplate past events. The reflection helped strengthen my inner self. It is an exercise which has helped me dwell on thoughts occupying my mind and resolve them. Like on any other day, I settled in my armchair in the open balcony as it neared sunset. The light was fading fast. Flocks of birds were flying to their nesting grounds. It is a regular sight in the skyline over the farm and repeats every day with clockwork precision. I stared at them, and my thoughts that day went back to my growing-up days.

I had lived in Madras for twelve years since arriving there after my school and escape from the turmoil of Calcutta. This covered most part of the eighties and half of the nineties. It was home to me now. I have never lived in any city for more than five years at a stretch and this was obviously the longest. Madras, now Chennai, in the southern part of India, is counted among the top four metropolitan cities in India. I had started my life in the new city by getting into university. The southern part of India had remained distinct from the rest of India for some reason – geographically because it is in the high plateau region, but more so because of a distinct culture, and distinct languages, traditions and physical features of the people. The rest of India did not seem familiar here. It was an alien world in those days when I had moved in. The spoken language, the written script, the smell of coffee, rice dishes and design of temples were all over, and different. They struck me as new. English was the language of choice over the national language, Hindi. While the rest of the country drank tea, southerners preferred their traditional coffee. This new experience gave me a fresh start, just as I had wished.

I fitted into the city and its culture. The city was cleaner and sparser, compared to Calcutta. With its almost desert-like hot summers and cool evening sea breeze, the weather was predictable. The longest stretch of the beach was the defining feature of the city. Everything seemed to be around it, including the exclusive residences, hotels, restaurants, shopping arcades, state offices and, most importantly, the university. I remember every moment of my experience. The visits to the British Council library, the charged-up games of cricket, long hours of friendly gossip, long cycling rides, and street-side cold sugarcane juice are some of the memories of my days in the city that I truly cherished.

While going through the paces in university, I was getting overwhelmingly convinced that I would go for a career of my own and would work for myself. I had picked up the word entrepreneurship then. It was a new word to me and it made me think. I remember I had discussed this among friends, but they did not seem a lot impressed. Most of them were inclined to follow the prevailing trend, seek out a good job and follow their peers. It is certainly safer to be doing what others have done. It involves lesser risk. In fact, for Indians, self-employment or entrepreneurship had never been a career option. I remember an incident published in a local daily. When at a convocation ceremony the university vice-chancellor was told that "his university is being known to give out the highest number of doctorates degrees", he said he "never knew which one of them will show light to the rest of them". I had cut out that piece of the newspaper and kept it in my file. To me then, his words hinted at entrepreneurship.

Aside from his insights, elsewhere, universities in general followed an age-old system of education, wrongly designed for entrepreneurship but rightly made for churning out foot soldiers. The system is geared to produce only workers, to fill stereotype jobs in bureaucracy, banks or the industry. A break from tradition was not visible to me then. True to the culture, campus interviews from corporate houses grew in numbers to attract new talent. It was a new phenomenon then, as corporate houses came looking for graduates, bringing with them promise of employment and, most importantly, a career. Many bright ones got through the interviews and relocated to other cities. Some even went overseas. Others took to appearing in various entry-level qualifying tests to get into the Civil Services, banks, insurance and various other jobs. Some took special tests to move out of the country.

Nothing had fitted my liking, and I waited for a way out. But the waiting on the campus was nearing end with the final semester running. I decided to take a chance and appear for a national qualification test for advanced studies. Qualifying would make me eligible for appointment as university professor anywhere in the country, or it would allow me to seek fellowship from the national grants body to conduct research and further my interest in science. What attracted me to this career choice was not any great lure of a job but the possibility of freedom to think freely, solitude and more time to spend with myself. I knew the financial rewards were the least in this path.

Months later, the result was out and I saw my name in the list. A morning newspaper had published the results. Seeing my name in a select list gave me an ecstatic feeling of success. I discovered my worth in science. I got busy in the next few days organizing my plans. Next would be to choose a university and a research program. I planned to simultaneously register for a doctoral program. The science subject I chose was not a highly decorated one, though. I say this as only one Nobel laureate was ever conferred a prize in this field. The winner, Norman E. Borlaug, was an agronomist and was conferred the award in 1970 for transforming world agriculture. My intent was not to look that far but to buy time for myself and to further contemplate. It was only then that I realized that I wanted to write.

*

A crackling call from a night owl somewhere nearby made me get out of my thoughts and sit back and try and spot it. I had nearly slept on my chair and had not noticed that the southern breeze was blowing and it had cooled the air. I had not seen an owl since I came here but had often heard it calling out. This one sounded very near. I had seen the carcass of a half-eaten animal in a corner of the roof a few days after my arrival here. I knew it was from an owl attack. I hoped I could spot the attacker today, and I did. Perched on top of the bamboo pole was a dark-colored owl, looking straight at me. The moonlight was enough for me to see its large eyes watching with intensity. I quickly identified the owl as a species of barn owl common to these parts. I felt good that I had company.

As I lay back once again, my thoughts went back to the past. Life in Madras was moving with a clock-work precision. I was working for a well-known chemical manufacturing company as a scientist. This was my first job, so I prized every moment of my working there. I had joined this company, as soon as I completed my doctorate program. In fact, I was not yet conferred the degree when the call came to work with them. A copy of the doctoral certificate was to be mandatorily furnished before the human resource manager, but for me it was waived for some reason. I started working in their newly opened research and development wing. To spend more time at work, I needed to stay closer to the office. Looking for a house was not an easy task in the suburban areas of the city. Those were times people built houses to live in, not to rent out. Apartments and mass housing projects were still in the phase of inception. People rarely advertised houses in the rental section of the daily newspaper. The only way to go about was by word of mouth, a good word of mouth.

During my search, a friend recommended me to a contact of his. On the day of meeting my prospective landlord, I was given an address. Upon reaching the destination, I knew this was not the locality I would be welcome in. The house was located next to a well-known temple. The owner of the house was the head priest of the temple and from the Brahmin caste. The place to rent was on the second floor of the two-storied building he owned and where he lived with his family. Brahmins in southern India practice strict vegetarianism. I am not from his caste and I can't think of a meal without a dish of fish or meat.

I knew this would never work and was a bit confused as to why my friend had sent me here knowing well my needs. Sheepishly, I knocked and was welcomed inside by the owner and his wife. I took a seat I was shown to. I quickly informed them there must have been some miscommunication in setting up this meeting. I did not want to go through the discomfort of prolonging the visit. The gentleman asked me what the miscommunication was about, as he had heard all about me from my friend. He had no objection to however I lived and whatever I ate. The talk was over even before it had begun and ended with a plate of hot snacks and homemade brewed filter coffee. Was this gesture of acceptance a new culture? A counterculture, I thought as I write now.

Living in this house, I completed four years at my first job. Work was routine. It was less about science and more of managing it. I was bunched with a group of people with a set of preconceived ideas and our only challenge was proving them right. I realized this as an unfortunate state for the subject of science. This happens all over the world, in small and large institutions, in the laboratory of the famous and not-so-famous, with scientists who are well known and those who still want to become known. There are two types of science – one is creative and the other, repetitive. To continue in both, sciences heavily depend on the number of repetitions or replications as vital proof. We have learnt that by controlling the sample size and the nature of the selected sample, it is often easy to get to the desired result. Eager journals pick this work and publish it. Copycat workers pick up such publications, envision further discoveries, and generate more research in line with it. Finally, they help strengthen theories, which eventually become established facts. Many poorly investigated ideas have through this channel become established facts. This is junk science, and I started realizing its worthlessness.

Science suddenly looked to me as a mere survival tool. One's growth in it didn't come because of originality but through skills of how one gathered contacts and connections. Though I could have kept working while maintaining my integrity, peer pressure was working against me. I soon realized I was not going to make much headway staying in a place that was fast turning into a "science ghetto". The hippie in me woke up and I was soon looking for a way out. I had the tools, and the internet. As the hippies went looking for an alternate culture, I, too, embarked on a new life.

4. Origin of Tussle

Life in a Small Town

The mind and body distanced from each other and failed to run together, unlike in my childhood days. In adulthood, I found myself lost. After childhood and the teenage years, I reached this phase which gave me the roughest ride. An intelligent body was now clouded by an always-present mind. I experienced a clear duality. Emotions crept in, ranging from anger to fondness, liking to hating, goodness to wrong-ness, and more. Emotions pushed the body to react. It often experienced confusing states – from elation to despair, wanderlust to inactivity. It was overloaded, trying to counter pressures and balance every mood. Often, I ran to seek solitude to contemplate and practice control.

The start of this phase put me on a challenging path. The stereotypical culture made me follow the others in seeking out a career, a mate, and a city to live in. One followed the other into a kind of blind alley, not knowing what lay at the end. There was no other way to a life and a "good-life" seemed all about getting them sooner, and better. The other way I was aware of was monkhood. It would turn my life, to give up family, devote myself to communal work, remain celibate, and live wherever work took me. Monkhood tests grit, determination and self-control in a manner nothing else does. No wonder it is revered and glorified in all cultures.

It leads one to instant personification, right from when one decides to step out of the commoner's path. Indeed, this option did strike me once but was gone in a flash, just as it had appeared.

Like my peers, I followed the road usually taken, but half-heartedly. However, looking for a career, and a life, in India was turning out to be an unforgettable experience. Now my curriculum vitae projects an aligned and gradual rise – but it fails to reflect all the toil. Every struggle is an unforgettable experience. In times of struggle, it felt like all the effects of gravity were bearing down on me. Every move felt heavy. The earth held me to the ground, but societal prejudices kept me from opportunities. Religious and caste biases were the most prevalent. I found it at every stage of my growing up and living years. The worst was when I filled my application forms for university education, and later for jobs in public and private institutions – I had to write my caste, religion and domicile. I saw this elsewhere, too. I haven't the least idea what purpose writing it would serve in modern India, when it is known that such information only created biases. I am, however, aware such information can be powerful factors, too, and will remain so for many millennia. There are places where it can help one get privileges. Elsewhere, they can lead to denial of basic rights. They count everywhere – while seeking jobs, securing a bank loan, making social alignment, and even in marriage. I often skipped writing them and sent confusing signals with my name, religion, caste and domicile. Once I was pulled out for an incomplete application form as I had purposely left the religion column blank. When such confusion occurs, one nearly becomes a nobody in one's own country. My intent was to stay above them. I was resolute that I would convince the system to think positively and inject modernity in their decision-making. It made me extra gritty and if it hadn't been for that, I would have been complacent and might have settled for much less.

My choice of a life path was, thus, determined. I knew very well I must juggle to make it all work. I somehow knew at the start that making a career, finding a place to live, a mate, and making these resonate as one in my life would be a challenge. This made me slow and indecisive. However, years of laboring finally brought me to all of them, but when it did happen, it came to me in disjointed form. It did not connect as one or a whole but stayed fragmented. Soon, I found myself doing a reverse. While people usually leave small towns and small jobs to live in big cities and do big jobs, I quit my cozy job and an easy lifestyle in Singapore to live in a small town in India. Friends termed my surprise move in different ways, some calling it "home coming", which did comfort me. Others called it "reverse brain drain", which elevated me. But I knew these were comfort words. To me, it was all circumstantial and more out of the need of my body and mind to remain together and mitigate my own suffering.

I was now living in Tezpur, a little-known place out of nowhere in the north-east Indian state of Assam. I came here accompanying my wife, who was assigned a new position in the town. Ten years of work in a few countries since leaving university with a PhD wasn't taking me where I wanted to go. I was on the lookout for a fresh start and needed time. There were also pressing personal issues, with my recent marriage playing a role, too, in my decision.

The town of Tezpur is on the banks of the mighty Brahmaputra, a river known for its vast muddy flood plains, wildlife and scenic sunsets. Originating in the Tibetan plateau, it hits the plains of India crisscrossing the states of Arunachal Pradesh and Assam before winding away and vanishing into Bangladesh. I was between jobs, so had all the time to explore the river's glory and the small towns along its banks. Amidst famed national parks and exotic locations, the stay was an experience I rejoiced in. The town also had remnants of ancient history, including artifacts of people living there a few centuries ago. Later, the colonizing British had made the town an administrative district headquarters and a strategic location during the World War for its campaigns in the East, particularly on the Malaysian peninsula.

I saw that over time the city was turned into a garrison for the Indian defense forces. Being close to the Chinese border, the place saw Chinese invasion in 1962. India had understood its strategic importance and was converting the city into a military base. With green military trucks on the roads and Russian-built Sukhoi fighter aircraft in the skies, the town was changing faster than any time in its history. Military camps were strewn across the town and in its suburbs. One would pass army trucks more often than civilian vehicles on the roads. It gave me a feeling of living on the frontline of a war zone, but, thankfully, all the activity was strategic and peaceful. The influx of the army gave the town an economic boost and transformed it into a bustling place.

I quickly made friends and found my way around. I picked up the local language and soon looked like a local at home. However, after the daily chores, my mind worked to find a way to restart my shattered career. I tried to apply to the local university for a possible position in research and teaching by setting up a meeting with the vice-chancellor but in vain. The university had its own system of recruitment and nothing seemed to have changed since I had left the country. Days turned into months and the right break eluded me. I had my savings but soon realized it would not last long. This worried me and made me clueless as to how I would restart.

Finding 'Buddha'

I had met my wife on an online marriage portal when I was in Singapore a couple of years back. It was a new phenomenon in India then. The website was suggested to me by a friend. I checked one such Indian site. In fact, it was started as a social experiment – a bright new phenomenon, where men and women posted their profiles, listing their likes and dislikes on an easy-to-search portal. Many of them had their pictures uploaded and some made it available on request. It was amusing reading the potential profiles. They often contradicted and some even mixed up their language. Some others expressed themselves so bitterly that it seemed they were not interested in the very purpose for which they were on the site. Castes, ethnicity, academic achievements, skin complexion, height, weight and food habits were mentioned. Theoretically, it came down to the understanding that you have to be a match, or a near match, to even start any correspondence. I didn't match with any, so my work was easier. My friends had found hundreds to work on for themselves and spent their prime-time hours on these searches. Often, a good find was discussed, others were trashed. It generated a great amount of energy and attentiveness. The hosting sites, to popularize an alternate culture and business, had unleashed their services. And, it was all free of charge.

The day came when I found my partner and soon we were married. I wrote about the matchmaking success to the portal in their feedback section to acknowledge their free service. It was the first time the portal had got an acknowledgement of this sort. A top newspaper contacted me following my feedback and asked my permission to use the information for their article, to be a sort of "cultural icon", a new generation person who went the digital way. I gave my permission and the article was published. It described at length the new social experiment and breakthrough in public perception. However, amusing as it was, the article ended quoting stories of mismatches, failure of expectations, and notes of caution.

*

People fall apart even after extensive courtship and cohabiting. Such reversible possibilities make going into a relationship a positive option. However, I believe marriage should happen once in life. When it happens, it changes a person, as it had changed me. It was the first time I was seeing another human so near me. That helped me understand more about myself. It was a period I said it all, did it all and behaved as truthful as I could. I opened up to my partner about who I was and what my orientation toward life was. While doing so, I also found out how different we were. I was aware that after all of this is shared, many fall out in their relationship.

Those who continue either agree, develop an understanding, respect each other, or are simply in love. The rest just stick together unknowingly, to use, to satisfy, or to nurture their respective egos. People sometimes come out of a marriage and marry a second time, but after that their outlook toward the relationship is controlled, careful and crafted. However, the whole exercise helps one understand who he or she really is. It balances one's opinion of oneself, which is often high and self-serving. Besides, all of this becomes a rich experience contributing to achievement of selfhood, as it did for me.

In his book *A New Earth*, Eckhart Tolle bares the complexity of relationships, saying "there is no true relationship".[1] He says: "It stems from the mere fact that in any relationship one is playing more of a role: role of being a spouse. This is not the real identity of a person. The moment the priest publicly asks 'Would you take someone as your husband or wife?' he has announced the role each has to play to remain in that relationship. What follows next are moments of role plays expected from the two parties. The pair's voice turns to sweetness, polite, loving and comfy, a total change from actual behavior when they are in the company of others. He explains further that "a range of conditioned patterns of behavior come into effect between two humans that determine the nature of interaction. Instead of human beings, conceptual mental images are interacting here. The more identified people are with their respective roles, the more inauthentic the relationship becomes".[1] And in time, one may hear a familiar voice demanding, "I never expected you will bring your cat along to stay with us." At that very moment, the chemistry of the relationship changes. Change in role-playing changes the nature of the patterned interaction and that is the start of the break in a relationship.

*

I got married in Cuttack, a historical city dotted with thousands of temples on the eastern coast of Orissa state. After living there for a while, we were moving to the town of Tezpur in North-Eastern India. The journey was nearly 2000 kilometers. We had to travel by rail and air. The train ride was from Cuttack to Calcutta, and onward to Tezpur by flight. We soon learned from the railway authorities that pets were not allowed inside the first-class passenger compartment. We had with us a six-year-old German spitz, the gentlest member of the family. We had earlier confronted the officials at the railway station over the rules. Surely, going by the book, Indian railways do not allow pets to travel in passenger compartments. It was soon settled that the pet would be isolated and would travel separately in the special caged enclosure in the last compartment in the rear end of the train. No one liked this idea, so I decided to travel together with the pet.

It was late afternoon when the train left Cuttack. I found myself sharing the cubicle with the on-duty master of the train. This cubicle was located in the last compartment, which was the freight carrier. I made myself comfortable on a wooden bench. There was also a single cushioned seat, obviously for the train master. I noticed the compartment had an attached toilet. This was a relief. In front of the single cushioned seat was a big black metal trunk which, it seemed, had items used by the master. The train rolled out of the station and in no time the landscape outside the window turned dark as evening fell over the countryside. With isolated specs of light coming from track-side habitations, I could not see anything. My eyes scanned the sky and through the thin December mist I spotted stars. They kept me company as the train swayed and cranked, piercing the darkness as it sped on.

A while into the ride the train picked up good speed. I shifted my attention to my pet, who had settled inside the cage and was pretending to be asleep. I knew he was not sleeping. It was his way of showing that he was bored and did not like any of this. The pendulum-like swaying movement of the last carriage and the steady loud clattering of the track was soon interrupted by a loud crackling sound of the radio. The two-way conversation over the radio suggested a possible slowing down and halt due to an accident on the route ahead of us. This would prolong our discomfort further. The guard looked much more disturbed and irritated by the news of possible delay. He stood at the door with his radio, staring into the darkness.

I settled into my thoughts to distract myself from the biting chill of the cold air blowing through the open door. My thoughts were about my present, its reality. I was without work. I had left my job in Singapore, despite persuasion from people around me. My new relationship was overwhelming me to an extent that it affected my daily functioning. A sense of guilt had crept in that made me believe I was not addressing the events properly. The only way to get over was to face the turmoil and deal with it. In the end, I had returned to India to find a resolution to it.

My thoughts went to the Buddha, and the reasons for his leaving home and the worldly pleasures to discover the definition of life and the cause of all the bundled suffering. All I knew about him until then passed me in a flash at that moment. A thought came spontaneously as I looked at the distant stars through the window and I wondered: "Why at this moment?" Am I seeking an escape from the events surrounding me? I was puzzled. I had never read about Buddhism in depth, but his decision to renounce the caged world to seek answers was well-known to me. His meditation, wandering life and inflicting pain upon himself have been epitomized. Out of his penance came truthful reasoning. Many have repeated his feat before and after for reasons various and plenty. The results varied, but the urge and need for contemplation and to take his path has never ceased.

My pondering thoughts were suddenly broken by the train master. Above the noise of his crackling radio, he said that I could get my pet out of the enclosure. He spoke again and this time he surprised me, saying he would be getting down at the next station and there would be a new train master taking his place. Importantly, he said I could go back to my cabin with the pet for the rest of my journey. Was this in any way an answer to my earlier thoughts, where I was looking for a way out of my present suffering? The train master's words were healing, though, for the moment because in him, I found my 'Buddha'. As I settled down waiting for the next station, the train passed through sleepy hamlets, over culverts and bridges and racing toward the east, and toward sunlight.

Fatherhood and Baby Semblance

Months passed living in Tezpur. Of all the days spent there, I remember one in particular. That night I was restless. I opened the window to look at the night sky. The sky had been my constant companion in those days. It acted as a chimney beneath which I often stood and vented my thoughts. The sky would reciprocate by changing its mood. I took its clear blue as a sign of righteousness. A puff of cloud was doubtfulness. The sky reflected many moods to me as I kept looking up. That night, from the bedroom window, I could see very little of the sky between the gently swaying coconut palms and neighboring building. What I saw wasn't much, but I saw a large, clear moon face peeping between the palm leaves. It was the middle of October and warmer than usual. The next morning, I was to take my wife to hospital for a caesarean section. The previous week, doctors had examined her and said the baby was healthy and safe enough to make a trouble-free exit, even though likely a bit early. The caesarean section was decided as she was mortally scared of the pain of giving birth in the conventional way and had refused to go through it, though I had thought it would have been an unmatched experience. I went with her wishes in a critical moment nearing delivery, knowing the many upheavals she was going through. Also, the decision to go for a caesarean process was a kind of selfish respite for me, as the nervous waiting would end sooner than expected.

Around 8 a.m. the next day, my son was born. Cocooned in his sleep, as in the womb, I saw him for the first time. Deep inside, I felt fatherhood in a way I could not describe it. It was like the completion of something divine, giving a new life a chance, a creation. I passed that moment of no sensation standing there as the entire cycle from start to finish flew past me in a flash. I didn't realize people were looking at me from around the crib for a reaction. I showed none. I was, too, overwhelmed. I looked at the baby healthy and hearty in sleep and it said all I wanted to know. The next two weeks were full of baby activities – changing, cleaning, feeding and, most important, putting him to sleep. Visitors came with wishes and gifts. In time, the baby grew strong and stable as care activities went on with precision.

On one of those days, while writing my journal I noticed that my diary had a Chinese calendar printed on it. Looking at it out of curiosity, I noticed that my son was born in the year of the sheep, just as I was. The revelation sent a momentary charge through my body. Indeed, only a sheep can be born to a sheep, I thought gleefully.

Another incident from that time was the constant mention by incoming guests about the resemblance of the baby. It was a big topic of discussion. All the time, the newborn was said to resemble his mother. Even though I could not find any such resemblance, I let them speculate. To me, the baby looked like any other baby. However, I thought it best to go with the flow as it would be a tribute to a mother if the baby resembled her. It would be a comforting acknowledgement for the mother who went through the arduous task of carrying.

As the baby was growing, his activities and demands became overwhelming to a point where the matter of baby resemblance thankfully came to be passed. However, the remarks of people on the subject stayed with me for some time. There had to be an evolutionary significance for it to occur, or nature would not invest in it. Later, while browsing some literature, I stumbled upon an article on baby resemblance in humans. It revived my tailing thoughts from the past. It was a research work published in journal Nature in 2005. [(2)] The study had put the same question I had on my mind to the test. The authors reported greater facial resemblance between one-year-old children and their fathers, than their mothers. Their argument was that a mother could be quite sure that the baby was hers no matter what it looked like, but the father couldn't be. Obviously, I was happy with this disclosure but remained puzzled as to why I had failed to notice the same myself. It was very recently when I decided to write this book that I found a more recent publication which questioned the first one and concluded the whole aspect of baby resemblance was a matter of chance.[3] To me this was a good find as it hinted progress.

Flying Business Class

Life after my son's birth was going grindingly slow. I had been without work almost a year and efforts to start a venture weren't happening as I had planned. Like on any other day, I had gone to the internet café to check emails, which I did twice or sometimes thrice a week. I didn't have an internet connection at home. Also, generally, connectivity was poor in this remote corner of the country. People with internet connectivity at home would complain that when they had connectivity, electricity would fail. We experienced six to eight hours of life without electricity in a day. This was routine due to shortage in power generation. It was frustrating, but somehow I had come to accept it all as anyone living in a small town would. The person at the café had by now become my friend and, knowing my intent, he was more than helpful. As usual, he gave me my preferred computer and seat. This computer was the only one connected to a printer, and he knew I often printed my mails. There were a few emails that day, but one brought cheer. An overseas company I had known long before was planning to start operations in South-East Asia and had been enquiring about my whereabouts after I had left my previous job in Singapore. They were gearing up to start their business venture with me. They wanted me to take the lead role and do the ground-breaking work. This was indeed the break I was looking for and it came when I wanted it most.

My entrepreneurship ideas which had frozen on the college campus were now thawing. I knew this was my opportunity and it was time to put my plan into action. The biggest challenge in setting up a venture was not how much I was going to make out of it, but how long I could sustain it. It needs a certain mind-set to be an entrepreneur and I think I had it. I was prepared for the unknown and was not aiming at the riches. The first challenge I had to accept was that I needed enough resources to run myself for months, or may be years. Second was to accept that failure was a fifty percent possibility. Third, there would be no vacation to look forward to. Very few people around me knew what this was all about, and I didn't have the time to explain. I just kept it simple for them – that I had finally got a job.

The next few days I made a plan, contacted people to organize my trip, and did my packing. I was going to the Philippines to make a start. The trip would be long. I would be travelling by rail from Tezpur to Calcutta, where I would stay for a few days at our family home. I would then proceed to Madras and from there secure my visa and fly out to Manila. It was time to say some serious goodbyes, as I would be gone for a long time.

It was a Malaysian airlines flight taking me out of Madras. While I was queued up to check in at the airlines counter, a duty manager stepped up to me. He singled me out from the queue and asked me to check in at the business class counter. First, I thought it was a decision to get the check-in done faster for people in the queue as the business-class counter was empty. To my amusement, I was the only one to check in this way, and to my greatest surprise I was handed a business-class boarding pass. I sat alone in the business class during the entire flight. Being the only passenger there, I enjoyed all the privileges – a welcome drink, plated meal and loads of chocolates, in addition to an attendant looking after me. I fail to understand why this happened. Was there a grand plan somewhere, associated with my intent? Upon landing, I mentioned my experience of privilege to many and their reply was in line with what had crossed my mind – it could only be a signal to a good start. I took it as a good omen.

Time with 'Michael Jackson'

Time flew immersed in my entrepreneurial work since I left India a third time now. From life in a small town, I had moved back to a bustling city. Philippines was my new home. The choice of the country, its proximity to all neighboring South-East Asian countries and its heritage as an English-speaking place and having friends favored me. Life was hectic. I was frequently traveling for business. Break from work was hard to come by, though a winter break in India was always on my calendar. It was usually the time to catch up with myself, family and friends, while everything around slowly came to a usual year-end closure.

It was just like any other December. I was in my farm early, enjoying the onset of yet another Indian winter. From my bedroom window, I watched the lazy sun rise over the distant tree-line in the morning mist. Over the chirping of multiple birds and the faraway sound of a farm tractor, I could do nothing except breath the morning air. My thought shifted to life, my life, its purpose; or was there a purpose at all?

Soon the much-awaited cup of hot tea arrived, with locally baked cookies on its side. In this part of Bengal, tea is always served with a siding. A cookie most often; in rural families it could be with a bowl of puffed rice or a baked chapatti from the previous night. I usually go downstairs to catch my tea while it is being brewed and poured into cups. Today, for a change, it was served in my room. The first sip had woken me up from my thoughts and brought the realization of me and my body. I was sipping the famed Darjeeling tea I had recently brought from my trip. Was it any different? Maybe. But what I was enjoying was the warmth it brought inside my body on a cool morning. It also raised me to the tasks of the day, and the week to follow.

I was to fly to New Delhi early the next day. The trip was hurriedly put together under some confusing circumstances. The best part was that I was going to see my son after a long gap. It was a culmination of several events and would give me a rare opportunity to spend time with him alone. He lived with his mother and grandmother. They would be going away for a few weeks and I needed to be around to baby sit. Though I felt the occasion was orchestrated for some reason, it served me good, as, for the first time, I would be living with my boy. I was not from his city and had never lived there more than a few weeks at a stretch. I was, thus, preparing myself for the unexpected.

My son was ten years old and living in New Delhi. The first hurdle I faced was getting up early to send him to school. It was a challenge in the freezing winter of northern India. The temperature was around 5 to 10 degrees centigrade for that week and there was hardly any sun to warm up. The city houses are not designed for winter but to withstand long and hot summer spells, which last six to eight months in a year. Wrapped in extra clothing and with room heaters, I tried to adjust to the bitter cold. But amazingly, the daily grind kept me warmer than any of my previous visits to the place. I needed to fix our breakfast and pack his lunch box every morning; it was an experience in itself. It was hard at first but turned joyous once I got a grip. The rest of the day went to regular chores, cleaning, cooking a lunch and waiting for my son's return. Evening was mostly sharing his school time and sitting through his homework. This would follow up with dinner and tucking him under quilts for a good night's sleep.

I enjoyed every moment of doing the household chores, which may be becoming irrelevant in the lives of fathers now. Looking at the people I know, I have felt this is happening in recent times. Men work hard toward getting a mate yet do not know much what to do with the child they father. Frank Putnam in his book *Man Enough: Fathers, Sons, and the Search for Masculinity* wrote: "For a couple of hundred years now, each generation of fathers has passed less and less skills, knowledge, wisdom and love to their sons. Over the same 200 years, each generation of fathers has had less authority than the previous one. The concept of fatherhood changed drastically after the Industrial Revolution. Masculinity changed hands from defining power to protect the family to going out and bringing money. Men stopped doing all the things they used to do inside the home. Instead, his primary role turned to bringing things into the family. This instantly turned him into an outsider. Consequently, he turned to conquer the world in pursuit of more, and yet some more. This forced them to go away for days, months and sometimes years."(4)

I have sat across the table many a time with friends and their families and the nervousness of the fathers was palpable each time. They never do their homework well anymore. They are never up-to-date with the kid's school work, the progress reports, the weekend picnic plans and upcoming birthday get-togethers. Somehow, they seem never to be a part of the family. This confused state had possibly made men look like nervous followers, and a talisman in modern families. My son rightly knew my weakness, so he provided me all the help I needed running through the days. I somehow felt children born to Generation X fathers are peace-loving and wiser than we were. We were go-getters, as life was explained to us as a limited thing, not limitless, as it is today.

One of the challenges I had taken up to prove that I was in full control of the situation was to find the right-fitting clothing for my son to look and act like Michael Jackson on stage. He chose to do this act at his school graduation day program. He was to do the famous "moonwalk", a dance step involving moving backwards while appearing to move forward. The step became popular around the world after Michael Jackson. As the day of the program neared, we scouted for the right clothes – jacket, classic shortened trousers, tie, white socks and hat. The challenge was to get the steps right and dress right. On evenings after school, he practiced to perfect his moves, with the music playing at full volume on my laptop and a set of mini speakers.

The final act on stage was wonderful and so were the accolades. To me, it was the completion of a task I had taken up and finished to my full satisfaction and joy. I also knew deep inside that I might not get another occasion like this with him. So, I cherished every moment doing what I did. On our way back, we celebrated our joy with a treat at a burger store. We even walked to his favorite ice-cream shack to enjoy an overly sweetened ice-cream in the bitter cold evening.

I sat watching him take his generous bites on the chocolate topping of his cone ice-cream and thought how he had started associating his happiness to his favorite items as he was growing up. He was never a demanding baby and loved his own moments. School took away most of his time and the remaining time was spent in home tuition, television, and the occasional sortie outdoors. As he grew, his environment changed. From a small town, he had moved to the bustling metropolis of New Delhi. He had enrolled in an upscale school. In those growing years, he found his happiness externally – in play items, eating out, and watching movies in theaters. At times, when he could not have these or if they were denied to him, he showed his irritation. His shoes and shirts needed to carry brand names favorably, or they were left unused or sparsely worn. Conformity to a set of invisible branding rules characteristic of urban society dictated his likes. Influencing factors were all around – television, magazines, advertisements, school and friends. As we walked across the mall and the bright lights of the outlets to the taxi stand, we passed crowds of ogling window shoppers. This is the changing dynamic of human happiness. Oblivious to this, young parents are bringing up their children surrounded by material things. Their reasoning for converting their homes to look almost like a mall is a sad indication of going in the wrong direction. The result of this gluttony is a generation of youth who are turning into nothing but consumers. As we drove back home through the maze of city shops and road-side stores, I hoped my son would soon get himself out of this unyielding web and free himself. He would learn to disassociate himself from materialistic things and seek joy in his life. I felt a sudden fear, a feeling of distress, disgust and helplessness all at once.

Living in Home without Walls

Growing up, I had realized I must start preparing to move out in search of educational and work opportunities. The body, which had been enjoying the comforts of a cozy home, would soon be tested. People who haven't left home or home territory will never know the hardship of parting. At the family dinner table, we often joked that those were the last few days I should be rejoicing a fine homemade meal. The next meal could be anything, anywhere. Consciously, the mind was being prepared for the venture away from home. I still remember my first journey looking for opportunities, and a career. I had completed my graduation and was called for an interview in Mumbai by the prestigious Tata Institute of Fundamental Research. I was then living in New Delhi. The journey was by train, the Frontier Mail. It was summer. The route had heavy passenger traffic. Mine was a last-minute reservation, so I had a seat in the second-class coach. As I did not have a sleeping berth, I must endure the long 30-hour hour haul seated all the way. I vaguely remember the sultry summer heat in the coach. Some respite was the train ceiling fan and whatever drinks the hawkers brought as they passed me frequently. But half way into the journey, it was announced that the train would not take its regular route as a goods train had derailed and tracks were blocked. Our train would take another route to its destination. The diversion would be long and would be an additional day's travel. By my calculation, I would be reaching Mumbai in the middle of the night the next day for an early morning interview. I also needed to find a place to stay at that hour in an unknown city. My making it to the destination would be a photo finish and it made me tense. This was my first journey to be part of the emerging globalization. However, the trip gave me more than a start. In a way, it opened up the world for me.

Since then, my body has enjoyed every trip I took across the world. I vividly remember many of them to this day. However, exploring the world physically was not part of my plan, though I ended up travelling the continents. Indeed, the earth seems to have suddenly contracted and become connected. While aviation connected me physically, the internet did it virtually. I made contacts and friends on every continent. It helped me understand people and their inner culture. I experienced the pleasure of friendship with strangers beyond the limits of commerce. I realized humans all over the world have similar lives, ambitions, goals, expectations and motivations. I experienced travelling to the interiors of China without knowing their language. A hand-held software that translated my speech took over my communication as I toured the countryside. I remember the benevolence of a Turkish neighbor turning up with no common language to communicate but with a big tray of breakfast early morning to make me comfortable. I cannot forget the safety net thrown around me in a city under siege in southern Philippines by my companion while we escaped the city. In Vietnam, I felt the warmth of a local technician who showed me around with his city on his rickety moped on a holiday, with nothing but hand signals. Similar experiences from other parts of the world are fresh in my memory. All of this shows humans can connect to make home away from home.

The human zeal to connect has created the global community we live in now. Ironically, it happened less through religion or faith and more through commerce. Benefits and rewards are what bind us stronger and faster than anything else. Commerce enabled by globalization has had many benefits. It presents choices, variety and, importantly, competition. It churned the economy and money flowed faster. A jewel craftsman in England is forced to get his best stone from India to stay competitive. So, it goes with all our goods in the market. Now we are connected and becoming part of the big Flat World 1.0 version, as said by Thomas Friedman.[5] He explains the transformation from version 1.0 to 2.0 of this Flat World with a quote from Dove Seidman: "We have gone from connected to interconnected and further to interdependent. So many people can now connect, collaborate and partner in much deeper ways. When the world is tied together this intimately, everyone's values and behavior matter more than ever, because they impact so many people than ever."

To look for the best, I traveled and made homes away from my home. I also shopped the best from around the world: chemistry from Poland, production from China, knowledge from the United States, opportunities from England, and partners from East Asia. It wasn't a distant land I had been after but an opportunity that was near, within reach. And this was made possible by connectivity and the internet. It brought the world to me.

The internet was in its infancy when I had started my first work in India. We could access it only in offices. Home connectivity was unthinkable and so was mobile access. Internet use was mostly for communication; I used it to connect with researchers far and wide. Their resources became my knowledge base. Physically making rounds of university libraries for literature and information was a dying trend and no more needed. I was gathering more information, and faster. All I needed to have were boxes of floppy disks to store the information. The world was getting connected and everyone's address was now an email, not a home with walls.

*

As the world evolved, everyone became a brand. I am reminded of my start-up incident where a venture I was prospecting was taking shape. It opened an opportunity for me to become a producer and manufacturer. I didn't have to go through the process of physical travel, and yet tasted my first big success. A company in Turkey had contacted me to produce a specific product for their market. I had the chemistry to make it but lacked the resources to produce it in bulk. To do the work I sought help from my contact in South Africa who co-owned a factory in China. The next few months passed sharing notes and updates. We spoke over Skype and viewed the process live. In six months, I transacted my first physical business, without having to meet any of the parties. This was outsourcing in a time when the word was not so common. The power of the internet freed me from the need to search for a home. It did put me on a path of wandering but of a different kind. My thoughts went back to the Buddha once again as a wandering monk. He never had a home, nor stayed in one place, but connected with the web of life and came up with dictums which hold steadfast even today.

5. Midlife Medley

Theory of Chaos

They say midlife starts at forty, and with it the challenging times. A term coined and commonly used to describe this stage is "midlife crisis". Crisis or not, it is the half-way stage through one's journey of life. From here, there is very little chance of turning back. In human life, passing the age of 40 brings one to that stage. It leaves many people bitter. At this point, most people would not change their profession, job, city they are living in, family, or acquired skills. Though little is proven about this stage and the state one is in at this time, it is the time when people may for the first time see signs of physical wear and tear, slowness, and a mellowing deep inside. It depresses many and sends them into a cycle of treatment and recovery.

At forty, I was nowhere – with a broken family, living separately, no fixed income, no place of permanent living and, importantly, looking for a meaning to my life. I was in a sort of backpack mode, living as a survivor. I was earning but was spending my earnings on my ventures, which had taken shape but had not solidified into assurances. In short, I had everything around me, but all of it lay incomplete.

Anybody in the perilous state I was in would have been nervous. I was in a state of chaos. But examining it now, I was probably in the right state then. Mine was the position similar to a master chef. I had all the cooking ingredients cut to shape and ready. The spices were measured. The cooking broth was extracted and the pan was in front of me. It was the time to light the fire and bring all of it together to cook a great dish. I am reminded of the theory of chaos while recollecting this moment. Authors Sheldon Kardener and Monika Olofsson Kardener in their book *Breaking Free: How Chains from Childhood Keep Us From What We Want* described humans as non-linear, open system.[1] In this book, the chaos theory provides an understanding of how new activity patterns can develop in prompt response to either familiar or completely novel stimuli. The greater the degree of flexibility a system has the greater its ability to adapt to changing circumstances. The theory is a balancing act between a totally deterministic world in which there would be no choices and a completely random world in which predictability of any kind would be impossible as there would be no way of making reasoned decisions. "If the behaviors in such an open, nonlinear system are neither random nor determined, how are they organized then?", the authors had asked. In fact, the chaos theory postulates that things are in fact organized around "strange attractors", which help us organize our thoughts, behaviors and actions. These attractors could be anything from religious beliefs, political system, one's training, to our childhood needs.[1]

I was in this chaos, surrounded by options, openness but looking for an organized outcome. From bright business ideas to a depressing domestic situation, from big business friends to shortage of funds, I was gambling on something to happen, trying to connect the floating dots. Nothing was making sense to me and I was unable to organize them into a worthy system. I was losing time. Strangely, rather than pressing ahead, I called a stop to what I was doing. I decided to get away from the muddle and take a long break. I soon packed up and went on trips, random and unplanned ones. The first took me to Thailand, where I spent a few weeks around monasteries, met an old friend and traveled around the countryside. The second was to Taiwan, again for a few weeks, doing the same. Next was to India. I wanted to realize the inner feeling of nothingness and nowhere-ness.

During these trips, I experienced lives of people first-hand. I visited universities and laboratories, museums and monasteries. One story which moved me during one of these trips as I interacted with a monk reflected the bitter ironies of life. Before being ordained as a monk, the holy man was in the police. He was a family man living in a city suburb. Having a "small" family, life should have been easy for him but turned out to be the other way. The constant demands of his wife and growing son for material possessions drove him to accepting bribes. The "extra" earnings kept his family members happy and content. But their demands kept increasing and they began drawing comparisons, saying, "Why others can have it and we can't?" He worked harder for his "extra" earnings to meet the new demands. But at one point, his conscience woke up and he could not rest any longer. His actions bothered him so much that he walked out of his house. He wandered around, confused and torn by his decision but found refuge joining a congregation, where he found companionship and, eventually, his own inner self. He is a contented man now and learning to remain so for the rest of his life. I never asked his name, nor wanted to know anything more. I will never see him again, but it taught me that it is possible to alter one's life to seek another with certainty.

During this trip, I also came across books introduced to me by friends and people who helped me interpret my life. I had never read books on philosophy and better living before, though I had a strong inclination toward the subject. Whenever the opportunity presented itself, I would go into lengthy discussions on the subject; but that was all. Coming across books on this topic was a first for me. Most of them were written by Western authors on a subject I had thought was the domain of Eastern thought leaders. A writer from a rich, successful and developed world contemplating life away from material and wealth was a new thought I had come to read about. I picked up many books, among them Eckhart Tolle, Robin Sharma, Richard Alpert, Deepak Chopra, Pankaj Mishra, Osho, and many more. They influenced me. I breezed through them, as if I was reading thriller novels. Each one was helping me find answers to my crisis. Eckhart Tolle provided respite to my wandering thoughts with his contemporary analysis and synthesis of Eastern spiritual philosophies, which had until then remained cloaked and complicated to me. One statement that had an almost miraculous effect on me was that "the primary cause of all unhappiness is never the situation but our thoughts about it". I closed and dropped the book. Why hadn't this realization come to me before? His statement pumped life into me. In fact, his reworking and interpretation of Hindu and Buddhist teachings, making them understandable, opened the faiths to me again. I had lost hope in my own religious books but now wanted to read them all. I bought copies of the Gita, the teachings of the Buddha, a Christian Bible and others to know what I had missed all these days. Soon, my crisis seemed to be under my control, and I hoped they would remain so.

Inside Courtroom

Getting a grip on the crisis did not at once make life easy, but it was a start to resolution of certain issues and a better life. My venture had taken a shape and was on track, indicating it would sustain. A number of writing assignments came my way. One was to write a book. I was on a clear path of fixing my work goals. There were also unpleasant matters to deal with. One such took me to court. I had never thought I would ever be in a court. But here I was, sitting in the lobby of the High Court in New Delhi, awaiting my turn to be called. I had filed for divorce, asking the court to annul the marriage on grounds of lack of fulfillment. It was January. It was chilly in the city but humid and warm in the courtroom. The crowd inside was uncomfortably large and noisy. Men and women in black coats and carrying folders and briefcases waited all over the cramped lobby, engaged in last-minute talks with their respective clients in hushed tones. I sat ruminating over the sequence of events that had brought me here. I was betting on my plea being judged in earnest.

I felt the institution of marriage had lost its solemnity in cultures from the day it was made near irreversible. I never considered this before tying the nuptial knot. I grew up under the romantic delusion, watching television, and reading pulp stories. Like my peers and pushed by culture pressure, I hurried through marriage as a task that had to be done, like any other task, fulfilling more of someone else's wish and racing against increasing age, weight and baldness. In order not to be among the left-behinds, and shunning negativity, I went through the motions, only to later turn up in court pleading. I looked around and saw similar stories of divorce and family disputes being played out in the room that day. The biggest losers in such contests are the children from these marriages. I could also see some youngsters about the lobby and wondered about my own child. To me, the emotion was long gone and the attitude was to get the job at hand done, just another of those jobs I needed to accomplish and move on.

The display screen was showing the list of cases to be heard that day. Mine was at number 7. I had nothing to think about at that moment. The incident that had led me to this place was known to the court. The court had insisted on seeing both of us in person to reach a settlement. I was told the judge was a lady and it led me to think the case would be judged differently.

Events of the past months had been unnerving, unfortunate and movie-like. A friend, after listening to it, joked why I didn't turn it into a script for a television soap. From quitting a stable job in order to save the marriage, living like a bachelor most of the time in spite of being married, trying to forego the hastily agreed mutual divorce pact in an attempt to rebuild the family for the sake of my son and, finally, distancing myself from my growing son to provide him peace – all this was too much of a sacrifice I had invested in this relationship. I had tried to live a balanced life, however impractical it might have looked. I was aware of my limitations and strengths. I was mindful that a cleansed living was near impossible, and my actions at times could be questioned on its goodness. But that is my truth, and I silently acknowledge it.

A relationship such as a marriage is an unnatural venture, which works on pure understanding. Warren Buffet attributed great marriages to the lowest expectation, not money, physical looks or anything.[2] But that's on paper. Often, it works and has its rewards, but most of it is about raw emotions and, at times, resembles a game of hide and seek. My decision to separate was the consequence of a series of recent events. Her activity, I knew deep inside, had made things unsustainable, and in some way disruptive. I could have acted or sought help to address what I felt was insensitivity on her part but waited for divine intervention. I never prayed in my life for personal gain and shortcuts. I always felt that every object or objective in this universe has an equilibrium, a state of finality, the attainment of which is eventual fate. The results may take time to show, but when it does it is nothing less than godly.

I had spent a few months contemplating and awaiting a resolution. And one day, it came. It was another of those nights and the last one I had passed clearing my head of past events. By dawn, it was clear – the relationship had ended and there was no room for me to endure it for any reason. It was a feeling of great relief, though the scene that followed was messy. Years of an on-and-off relationship is not easy to erase. This is the same story I presented in the court in seeking a new beginning.

Found Peace in My Writing

People are mostly finished planning their new venture in midlife, but I was exploring new possibilities and options. This was the time my body and mind ran in cohesion once again, as in childhood. Humans are made to explore. Not mere physical exploration but in the mind as well. While the body is limited physically, the mind has the capacity of boundless imagination. No day passed without exploring. It often became a pastime. Each effort was toward discovery, innovation, betterment and productivity. Venturing into them brought unity, cohesion and restfulness within.

I was exploring how to break into writing, to be a writer. I had ideas but never had the space and time to write. People mistakenly think writing is to gain fame, name and money. It wasn't my intent. In fact, very few writers gain these despite working their whole lifetime. Yet, they continue to write. My all-time favorite author Khushwant Singh explicitly explains in his autobiography what it takes to become a writer. I am in total agreement with him. He says: "To become a writer one needs the compelling passion to become one. Motivating force is not money, as there is much more money elsewhere, nor the quest for recognition or fame, which again lies elsewhere. As a matter of fact, most writers have no idea why they took to writing, except for some kind of inner urge which compelled them to do so. In most cases, the urge abates when they discover that it takes a lot more to translate desire to become a writer into actually becoming one. The urge comes again and again until they find an outlet."(3)

I was now getting the inner pangs, as if I had set an alarm in my body clock. I was trying to shut these alarms by excusing myself. In fact, I had no idea how the publishing industry worked and I never encountered a writer in my life to guide me. Now that I would find my own way, I was resolute. While the head worked on how to go into this new venture, the body would stay still and let the mind work. I often looked for privacy and seclusion, so as to keep to myself. I would find a silent corner in the café, or in a lobby while waiting. Sometimes, I would leave office early to spend time at home, or take time off to go to a new location and lock myself in the quiet surroundings. I was behaving like I was possessed.

I soon decided I would focus my first venture and write a book on the subject I professed. I knew the field. I also knew the audience. I had a need, too. I came up with a theme, a more contemporary subject matter which would appeal to the publisher. It took me a while to put this together as I had to do a good amount of reading and literature review to keep myself abreast of the current science around the world. Once I was happy with the subject, I drafted the content with an index. Once done, I wrote a letter of intent and submitted the draft to three top publishers of scientific books in the world. I do not recall how long I had to wait for a response, but when it came, it brought a hint of a possibility. I was sent a long questionnaire to fill up. The questions were a mix of scientific queries, which I could very well explain. The challenge was answering questions about my credentials and marketing related matters. I got down to research and find the answers. I had to suggest names of five well-known referees and their most recent status. It would be used by the publisher to generate opinion. Everything done, I waited.

*

The books I have come out with generated interest in the audience it was intended for. Strangers walked up to me at conferences and meetings to acknowledge my work. Whether I made money out of it or whether it put me on a pedestal, mysteriously remains unknown to me? I had kept this distance intentionally. What the books have done to me is it brought me to a near meditative mode when at work. It brought my body and mind together through intense focus and concentration. I felt the focus, the energy and clarity. The clutter around me had vanished. A yogic atonement set in as I worked. And, it took care of the many years of my midlife and stalled the onset of the dreaded “crisis”.

6. Search for Identity

To be Born as a Human

The question of who I am and why I am here has been inside me since my university days. The urge to find answers grew with age and experience. It is a question Eastern cultures have been asking themselves since time immemorial. However, its relevance in the contemporary world has grown as Eastern philosophies have come to be accepted in the West and have gone global, too. Ironically, the pathway of self-reckoning and tools of a "good-life", though discovered and penned in the East, returned to the East after it went through a process of retrofitting in the West. Meditation and mindfulness are Eastern concepts, but only after the West accepted them did the East come to see it as a popular and urban way, a signature lifestyle. This happened as the Eastern urbanite realized that wealth and development can go along with meditation and mindfulness. Earlier, most people in the East had never accepted these concepts as they had wrongly viewed it as a sign of non-progressiveness, and distress.

I believed self-discovery is a critical path to understanding oneself. This path leads to finding the purpose of one's earthly life and connects the mind to the body. It helps one integrate with one's surroundings. Those who seek answers and get them are the conscious ones. Such people hold the key to the future of humanity as they find unity with the world, especially the natural world, and transform themselves into being creationists, conservationists, rationalists, and even revolutionists.

What triggered my search was my own state of being restless at rest, and miserable with comfort. I was living in a precarious state. It was then that the question of who I am and why I am here crossed my mind. I clearly recall the countless nights I had spent staring up at the night sky to connect the loose dots and find answers. I traveled to places and experienced mountains, spent time by jungle streams, trekked to sulfurous craters and camped in rain forests to understand the essence of life and this living body. I researched and collected books on Eastern and Western philosophies and listened to recorded speeches of Western preachers and Eastern gurus. They all generated thoughts and insights in me, but somehow, they were not making any deeper sense. When I read, they conferred meaning, but then they vanished as effervescence. They all seemed to miss something somewhere for me to find a grip.

Looking for who I am and what I am may sound self-centered. But being self-interested is the beginning of knowing oneself. Evolution taught us to run when chased by a hungry predator. We had done this to prevent ourselves from becoming meal. Inside a plane, we are instructed to put on our oxygen masks once they drop down, before we help a child put them on. Instinctively, many would do the reverse, as it would be selfish to think about oneself before one's child. The sublime distinction in these acts is that they are designed to save us first. Only if one can save oneself can one save the rest. The very thought about oneself is the beginning of self-identification. It is the realization of the body. Selfishness would have started as a method of survival for the body. The body does not understand another body. The body's intelligence is purely to self-serve. However, it is justified to condemn selfishness as negative when it enters the mind.

Evolution of Human

I am just one life among countless other life on Earth. It may sound an insignificant thought but, in a cosmic sense, it is nothing short of a miracle. We haven't found life anywhere else after many explorations deep into space and the universe, though the elements needed for life to exist are present in many places out there. This made me think life is nothing less than a spectacle. It is, in fact, much more, looking at the mere fact that I, too, am a human life, whose story if considered as a single volume, we actually know only the last page of, as rightly described by Tim Radford in his article in the Guardian.[(1)]

What is unknown is how we came to be and what transpired, so we have become as we are today. Evidence points to our possible link to apes. Most forward-thinking religions have accepted this theory. Nobody has witnessed this event, but skeletons discovered scattered across the explored land indicate a gradual transition and branching six million years ago. These are anthropological evidences in the form of skeleton remains of forms, suggesting a link between apes and humans at various stages of transformation. [(1)]

The best, however, comes from genetic analysis showing that humans are genetically near match to chimpanzees. This signifies Darwin's evolutionary theory which replaced God with an ape as the originator of humans and shocked many. Tim Radford, in the same article, went on about the biological semblance that has led to the evolution of certain shared behaviors in humans and chimpanzees. He writes that "chimpanzees struggle for status, vocalize, communicate, play politics, use subterfuge, show aggression, reject outsiders, groom and support each other, betray each other and resort to violence or sexual bribery to get their way. Chimpanzees display awareness of self, ability to reason, and a grasp of numbers. Chimpanzees are opportunistic omnivores that also make and use tools for gain, and groups of chimpanzees in the wild have separate traditions, practices and ways of doing things that they pass down the generations. Chimpanzees have some culture". However, we have a handful of chimps left in the wild, and a land full of humans. This clearly shows our power to overcome and manipulate our environment. Could this be the last leg of a relay race where the evolutionary baton was passed on to the humans by the chimps to run the final stretch, while they stayed on track to watch us win?

It was on a business trip in South Africa that I got an opportunity to visit the 'Cradle of Humankind', a must visit museum in Maropeng. I had heard about it but never had the chance to see it during my past visits to the country. This time, we bunched up with fellow business attendees and traveled to the most sacred of all spots for humans. To me, this is the holiest of holy sites. Many hominid, or human-like, skeleton remains were discovered in the limestone caves in this region. Many still lie buried, undiscovered to this day.

After an hour's drive from Johannesburg, we reached the place. The expanse of the landscape was striking – a vast stretch of grassland dotted by a few trees. As I stood, leaning on to the railing at the viewing point overlooking the open landscape, my thoughts went a few million years back. Small groups of hominids, pre-humans, had lived here in that time. We were an uncharacteristic form of animals in the landscape, capable of perfect bipedalism, with hands freed from locomotory functions to perform complex tasks. Devoid of sophisticated tools, fire or clothing, we were vegetarians and lived by gathering our food. The rest is history – Man evolved into a cultural animal and went beyond Nature's control, to explore possibilities.

The theory of evolution of humans from an ape ancestor was never easy in Britain when first proposed in the eighteenth century. Richard E. Leakey and Roger Lewin gave a fine account of the situation in their book, *Origins*: "On hearing one June afternoon in 1860, the suggestion that mankind was a descendant from the apes, the wife of the Bishop of Worcester is said to have exclaimed – My dear, descendants from apes! Let us hope it is not true, but if it is, let us pray that it will not become generally known." But the Judeo-Christian theory of Creation, nearly two millennia old, did not accept this easily. It was a reassuring thought that God created Man, all at one time in the modern shape of Adam and Eve, and that we are their descendants. In the first ever Creationists versus Evolutionists debate during the annual meeting of the British Association for the Advancement of Science held in Oxford in 1860, Bishop Samuel Wilberforce asked Thomas Henry Huxley sarcastically: "And you sir, are you related to the ape on your Grandfather's or your Grandmother's side?" Huxley's reply, though philosophical, marked the era of our earliest known Renaissance. He had replied: "If I had the choice of an ancestor, whether it should be an ape or one who having scholastic education who used his logic to mislead an untutored public, and should treat not with argument but with ridicule the facts and reasoning offered in support of a grave and serious philosophical question, I would not hesitate for a moment to prefer the ape."(2) Evolution won that day and has since accumulated facts which helped place humanity as a part of the earthly environment, not a bolt out of the blue sky.

Eventually, humans came to be identified as primates but with a typical culture. Take away the culture and the animal could be described as anything from what Plato said: "a two-legged animal without feathers", to what Mark Twain said: "the animal that blushes or needs to".(3) From outer nakedness to our emotional attributes, we are truly a unique bunch. But what truly defines humans is the way we live, with a series of invented things such as values, ethics, beliefs, and, of course, tools. These have come to dictate our lives to an extent where humans are transformed from an animal to a cultural animal.(3) Culture further divided us into groups and subgroups within our own kind, each differing in physical looks, ethics, beliefs and other aspects.

Human as Cultural Animal

The animal part of humans is also unique, like no other. A naked skin defines us most of all. We are also defined by a tuft of hair on top of the head, underarms and the pubic region, prominent eye whites or optic sclera, enlarged and pendulous penises, enlarged female breasts and a few more to count.(3) Each of these features is truly human and has been further improved to make us stand even more apart from the rest in the animal group. Skin is now waxed and polished, the remaining hairs pulled out to look more naked. Hair on the head is cut, curled, grown long, colored, tied and combed in style to look special. Dresses are designed to enhance bodily features in the name of styling and trend. These features, however, hold appeal and significance, as they play a role in self-presentation, in boosting confidence, and while making selections, such as in mate pairing. However, it is the culture part of humans which possesses the greatest diversity. It is impossible to separate the cultural aspects of human existence and study the biological aspects separately. Some contemporary scholars suggest that the human condition might best be called "nature/culture".(4)

I recall an incident from long back, when I had a glimpse of culture at play. While at university, we would debate on a number of topics. One was, women. From their looks to character, every aspect was debated. And why not? It was the time we men on the verge of breaking into careers wanted to know the skills of choosing a future mate. From arranged marriage to the less practiced marriage outside communal and caste lines, everything was in question. I remember the opinions were very varied and could have been divided into clear groups. Men from the city and those from small towns and villages had divided opinion on arranged marriages. City folk made clear they would marry women of their choice, irrespective of economic, religious or caste considerations. While the other felt they would marry from their respective communities according to their parents' choice. It was an interesting subject for me, and I took it to my course supervisor as thesis subject in the field of animal behavior. He disagreed, and I ended up studying spiders and their mating behavior.

Culture plays a big role in showing human behavior as dependent on the society one has grown up in. That is why anthropologists travel the distance to study original human behavior in indigenous societies, that is, natives or aborigines. The assumption here is that these societies might be the only remaining representation of original human life and behavior on Earth. The expectation that all non-European societies express human nature more naturally has been thought to be the way to know more about the human condition.(3) Such societies are thought to be devoid of what has now come to be called common human culture.

An example of cultural influence on popular notions about humans can be seen in an interesting aspect of human mate pairing behavior, as explained in an article citing a study. The study was conducted on men, who by nature get attracted to women. When men were shown silhouettes of women, they were seen to be most attracted to women with waist-to-hip circumference ratio of 2:3.(5) A critical observer might note that the 2:3 ratio, or 36-24-36 in inches, is the glamorized figure of Hollywood starlets and wonder whether the male preference was actually evolved human nature or simply a reflection of the universal exposure of people to the values expressed in modern media and movies.(3) To test this hypothesis, anthropologists, asked the same questions about their preferences of women's figures to a short, stocky group of people known as the Matsigenka, who live high in the Peruvian Andes. They found that, contrary to the uncritical assertions about human nature, the Matsigenka men preferred women shaped just like their own women are shaped, and not like Marilyn Monroe.(6) A study among the Hadza people in East Africa gave a similar result. Thus, what seems to be a "universal preference" is after all an expression of globalized culture, not of human biology.

This gets more interesting when we examine another aspect of mate pairing in humans: that "women widely prefer wealthy men as partners". The researchers proved that this claim is only true in places where women are denied access to resources or property.[7] It shows that the environment overwhelmingly influences human decision-making and behavior at all times. So, it is nearly impossible to know what humans truly represent. In a way, we can simply say humans are cultural animals. Their thinking process and behavior merely represent their culture, not biology.

Religion as a Culture

Humans have developed and nurtured thousands of cultures by now. Each group is different from the other in opinion and decision-making. Religion is one example of such dominant culture. Religion is a man-made path where most humans put their faith in and make it their way of life. From the cradle to the grave, religion dictates human life. Newer countries like the United States of America, a country of immigrants and a free nation, are known to be predominantly Christian. However, today, in a short span of 200 years of its history, the country is estimated to have over 2500 religious cults with thousands of members in each of them.[8] These cults have devised their own beliefs and ways, often cutting off themselves from others using drastic means and methods. Some have made news headlines for reasons such as their amassing guns, mass suicides, sexual overtones and more.[9]

Cult culture, or cult-like culture, exists in most major religions. Humans are drawn to it with the promise of Utopianism, egalitarianism and a life of free will because mainstream religion failed their expectations and looks to be less rewarding. It intrigues me what makes modern humans fall prey to superfluous cult groupism. The fear of being left out, or to gain power? Once I was approached by a member to become a part of such a 'group'. He promised I would enjoy contacts and connections and rise socially. I had then quipped: "It made sense to me, but the ideology of the cult, the do's and don'ts, how am I going to accept those? And I may disagree with them." His answer was very reassuring: "To get something, you have to lose something..."

I have come to know people who join groups to derive benefits. Everything seems to be available, from tax exemption to a bed in heaven. In addition, humans are animals with the most amount of fear. Fear of persecution, excommunication, deprivation and being left out bothers them all the time. But if people join these groups, there must also be someone who forms them and leads them. Who are these individuals? Are they supernatural, gifted, mystic? I researched and found origins of many such groups and putting all of them together the story goes somewhat as described here. A hungry, wandering, distraught man found a scenic spot on the banks of a river. He set up camp there. He sat in a meditative posture for a reason known only to him. In three days, everything he wanted was in front of him. He had food laid out before him and visitors thronged from far and near with gifts. In no time, he had followers, and later a group. He gave the group a mystical and divine sounding name to make it appealing to the masses. Soon, the masses followed him, and worshipped him. Masses drew politicians, which in turn drew the television. He soon rose to be an influential person and the story of his power to change people's lives spread far and wide. But his body did not understand the plot. The last I heard of him was that he was in jail on charges of exploiting women. His followers continue to deny the charges against their guru, claiming they are politically motivated by a rival group to cut his influence.

What eventually happened to the guru is not my interest. The point is, there is immense power in common interests and desires of humans to bring them together. They had come together under a guru, maybe to dispel their fears and feel protected. The above incident happened in India among an illiterate, poverty-stricken community, where people are desperately looking for miracles to bring change in their lives. Similar groups have evolved and flourished around the world, including in developed countries. Group most known are for religion and for politics. Hitler's rise to power is an example of the immense influence of common people and their personal experiences, which eventually conferred authority to him, as explained by Yuval Harari in his book. He goes on to say, "Hitler was a mere corporal in the army with no education, no skill, no political background, not an activist, no connections, not even a proper citizenship. Then, the reason for people electing him to power is a fascinating subject of leaders in the making."(10)

How Social is a Social Being?

I have disliked joining groups of all kinds and this has been always the case. The feeling of being part of a group never appealed to me. The only group I had voluntarily joined was the sports team in school and at university. But these are easy groups as they get disbanded in less time. In another instance, the closest I came to being part of a group culture was my short stint on Facebook. I was attracted more by its privacy settings and options. I had created the account to share my travel photographs among chosen friends. This adventure was short lived as my benign intent was infringed by popular pressure to include my personal life into it. It had annoyed me and I shut my account, never to return.

The groups which I am fearful of are the ones which claim to leave a legacy. I have shied away from cultures, starting from small neighborhood societies to complex multi-layered organizations. Their manifesto and ideology do not appeal to me. The ideas they present are never wholesome. They have hierarchy, need influence, and are motivated by rewards. These set-ups are opinionated and can never be called independent. I remain wary of each of them.

I have strongly believed one cannot be called a true visionary if one works for someone or represents a group. The culture of a company or group we associate with could greatly influence our perception and worse still, our action. I have never pledged allegiance to any group or organization. I have never been attracted by any dogma and have remained independent as much as possible.

My venture for independence remains an experiment on myself. This freedom allowed me to judge an action by its wholesomeness and rationality. It also allowed me to be strong to judge people critically. I remain keen to know the person more than the culture that person carries. I have always wished to meet and hear the person talk, not where he or she belonged to. This has made me conscious about the presence of humans around me all the time. It came to me naturally. I encounter people regularly and they happen to be associated with business, or are friends, family and relatives. I also come across strangers in my work, through email, and in personal life. Every time I interact with them, my actions are specific and with a purpose. This is most obvious, though not all my interactions with people have a value attached them. I have noticed I use certain innate tools to rate a person and check if he or she has certain characteristics or not – characteristics which make them likeable, or my type. I have found three parameters I generally tend to use. This has worked with a great degree of accuracy and made me feel comfortable in judging people. One parameter is whether they can cook, or have the inclination to. Second, their love for animals. Third, if they read books. Those who fulfil these, I feel are my type.

I am not sure what is contained in these three very different evaluation parameters and, importantly, how it had occurred to me to use them in my judgment. I have given a significant amount of thought to this phenomenon out of mere curiosity. I think people who cook or show interest in cooking are more natural and spontaneous individuals. Their primordial need to look for food or fix a meal sounds as security to me. Love of animals or pets such as dogs come naturally to most humans. Human babies, from the cradle to school, have stuffed teddies as playmates. Animal cartoons engage kids most of the time. Later in life, stuffed cuddly animal toys or live pets are exchanged as gifts to express happiness, joy and love. Those who avoid or hate dogs must have had some type of abnormal childhood – disruptive family or unknown phobia, rare among humans. Books are my favorite items and I have had them since learning the alphabets. I collected, read and tried my hand at writing all my life. However, there might occur exceptions to this rule, and that is the core of human culture.

Humans love the joy of living socially. The basic groups are usually relatives and closely related members. Often, these groups go beyond relatives and may involve outsiders. Apart from sharing common goals such as protection and help among the group members, humans are also known for displaying remarkably good behavior, which is often intriguing. They include behaviors such as donating blood or organs to save strangers or, at times, throwing themselves into danger to rescue fellow humans. I remember recently watching the footage of a Malian immigrant in France climbing up to the fourth-floor balcony to bring down a child to safety. Sometimes such human acts lead to loss of lives while trying to save another. In such situations, the body assesses the danger and checks on the action to be executed. The mind, however, rushes ahead to accomplish the task. The body does not understand the meaning of dying for glory but is overwhelmed by a charged mind to accomplish the task. This altruistic behavior makes humans more than just social animals. The instinct to throw oneself by a stranger's side lies deep in most of us. What drives us to such actions? Are these actions triggered by a sense of reward, or to derive pleasure from accomplishment, or competition to be on top?

I have studied eusocial organisms such as ants, termites and bees in nature and in captivity. Each exhibits cooperation and group bonding to care for their offspring, defend nests and scout for food. The group behavior has been taken to such an extreme level in these social insects that they have developed something of a caste system, where one group has given up all reproductive power and devoted their entire life to nursing and raising the young, while the other 'caste' specializes in defense, defending the nest against intruders. The responsibility of mating and producing eggs is with another 'caste', anthropomorphically termed kings and queens. Each colony defends its territory from another colony of the same species. But group interaction and cooperation are also notable. It is inferred that there must be an evolutionary reason for such cooperative behavior among non-related members, just as in humans.

In his book *The Social Conquest of the Earth*, Edward Wilson describes humans as eusocial apes. He sets humans apart from other living apes and the many hominids that either preceded us or coexisted with us, and are now extinct.(11) Eusocial would mean humans are truly social beings. This brand of extreme behavior has acted both as a blessing and a terrible curse.(11) Natalie Angier, while reviewing the above book in the Smithsonian magazine, wrote: "Experiments have shown that it is shockingly easy to elicit a sense of solidarity among a group of humans who happen to be strangers. Just tell them they'll be working together as a team, and they immediately start working together as a team, and are prepared to do battle against those who fall outside the team. In experiments where psychologists divided people into groups of arbitrarily assigned traits, such as one set as the Blue team and the other one as the Green, the groups started sniping at each other and expressing strong prejudices toward their "opponents", with the Greens insisting the Blues were untrustworthy and unfair. This innate drive to form and take deep pleasure from in-group membership easily translates at a higher level into tribalism."(12) Wilson states "this can spark religious, ethnic and political conflicts of breath-taking brutality".(11)

Edward Wilson examines this human condition in depth and explains that the power to form groups quickly, or the "phenomenon of groupism", has, in fact, led humans to a type of struggle, a struggle of "us versus me". He wrote that "humans are playing a kind of mixed economy with a complicated process of multilevel selection all the time". This means "some of our impulses are the result of individual selection, which is the competition of individual against everybody. This includes sharing of life's goodies. On the other hand, we also behave altruistically for the sake of the team or a group we represent. It appears our individually selected traits for basic life goodies are older and more primal, and harder to control. These are traits that we traditionally label as vices, such as greed, sloth, lust, coveting neighbor's life, and pride. On the other hand, our eusocial inclinations are evolutionarily newer and more fragile and must be vociferously promoted by the group or community if the group is to survive. This is enabled by religion, a political party, or affiliation to a social or environmental group. This also includes characteristics such as virtues we admire: generosity, kindness and level-headedness, controlling our impulses, keeping our promises, and rising to the occasion even when we are scared or disheartened".[12]

*

Considering all the above, I will refrain from calling humans just eusocial. We are naturally oriented to look for the best for ourselves before the greater good of our species. The term eusocial should be reserved for ants, termites and bees. Humans would need another description, far greater in flexibility and which will suit us best. Our culture is naturally inclined to be unnatural, as Wilson puts it rightly: "The worst in our nature coexists with our quest for the best, and so it will ever be."[11] It points to our zest for competition and pursuit toward becoming the fittest human among humans as our true identity.

7. Answers in Culture

What it Means to be a Hindu

What am I seeking? What is best for me? Can I single them out? I thought of an answer to this question that will eventually help me know myself more. At the same time, it will put an end to my restless mind. However, I soon realized what I am seeking is deeply embedded in my culture. The culture I grew up in provided all the basic motivation for what I was seeking. The religion I grew up in interpreted all the actions around me, the country of my birth influenced my perspective about the world, and the people with whom I lived influenced my life mission.

Humans, however, live their lives unmindfully driven by reward. We grow up centered around a process of give and take. All our happiness and suffering seem to be revolving around a prize. "Rewards shape our behavior," wrote authors Jamil Palacios Bhanji and Mauricio Delgado. They further explained: "Out of a vast space of possible actions, the prospect of a reward helps us select those actions that will lead to the most and best rewards, and motivates us to carry out those actions."(1) This looks unsustainable right at the start. In fact, religion evolved all over the world to delink humans from this primeval association. In Chapter 4, verse 20 of the Hindu book of *Gita*, it is said: "Being detached from the fruits of action, being always satisfied and independent, he performs no fruitive action, although involved in many activities."[2] Same is said elsewhere by other religions, but human nature and the underlying culture rules above all. Modern living has pushed us further toward rewards at every turn, making religious philosophies near obsolete.

I was born in India into a Hindu family and was initiated with a Hindu name. The name created my first identity. It contained my gender, ethnicity, linguistic group and religion. My father had picked the name of a mythological character from the Hindu epic Mahabharata. In the years I was growing up, I listened about this person, "Parth", his mastery, valor and more. I also read the Hindu mythical story where he features as an archer, a soldier and, finally, as a student recipient of the divine dictum from the Lord Himself. Mahabharata is a Hindu epic composed hundreds of years before Christianity and Islam came into existence. There are other epics as well and to me these were attractive fables, with adventure, action, thrill and romance. It contained good and bad acts, jealousy, joy, sacrifice, loss, devotion, deception, revenge, love, lust and more. It exemplified human nature, reminding us what we are truly. This was my initiation, which no one could have imparted to me but Hinduism.

Humans are a cultural bundle. Author Jonathan Marks described it in an article: "Human phenotype is both the proximate and ultimate product of culture as well as of DNA."[3] Thus, human behavior, attitude and interpretation express the environment they are born into and raised in. Even though we grow up consuming the same baby food and learning alphabets in the same school, our perspective remains distinct, and at times distant. Result of this is my identity as a person is also the culture to which I belong. I have come to believe that a big part of one's culture is the ethnic group one is born into and the religion one is identified to be practicing. A Hindu Punjabi, a Turkish Christian, a Russian Jew, an Arab American are all expressions that confer a certain identity and action to a person. Irrespective of the place they were born and raised in, they would carry a distinct culture of their inheritance with them.

True to this, a big part of me is my religion. However, my being a Hindu has often been a difficult part to explain. I can boldly say I am not religiously circumcised to be a Catholic or Muslim. I do not wear long hair or uncut beard to be a Sikh. I am allowed to enter and attend ceremonies in a church, mosque, synagogue temple or monastery. I am allowed to eat all types of food, raw or processed, if it is cleanly cooked and served in a group. In Hanoi, my business contacts once tested me by thrusting at me a glass of cobra blood in rice wine. It was a hallucinating drink for a group initiation. After I had gulped down the drink, their laughter-filled remark "Are you really an Indian Hindu?" explained what being a true Hindu is all about. I had accepted to go through this process not to prove any point but to eat other people's food to know them better. I have had whale meat in Japan, pork blood meal and unhatched duck eggs in the Philippines, snake meat in Vietnam and insects in Thailand to let people around me know that I am one among them. I did all this consciously, in the absence of a camera or a crowd. This is the organic nature of my religion, Hinduism.

I am a Hindu by not doing what the rest of its followers or faithful do. I am a Hindu by mere default. When a group of local missionaries walked into our home in Chennai to introduce gospel teaching, they were surprised to find a cross in our living room. I had bought the clay sculpture from a roadside store and had hung it in the room. I even gave it a fresh coat of paint as it had faded over time. In Turkey, I had sat down on the floor and shared a communal meal served on a single large plate. I ate with my hands, helping myself to chunks of rice and meat from the plate. I drank a yogurt drink called "airan" from a common brass jug and also took a puff from a communal hookah kept there. It was a local celebration and I was invited to it. The others went into the neighboring mosque to pray, leaving me at a park, where kids played. We later parted with customary hugs and kisses, as if I was one of their own.

During my deepest crisis days, I had sought guidance and solace in Buddhism. I traveled and read as much of its teachings as I could. I visited monasteries in northern India, Thailand and Taiwan. I chose Buddhism over the rest because of its origins, and its link to Hinduism. Also, Buddhism is recent, clear, subtle, and has overwhelming influence in South-East Asia, where I live. Being a Hindu allowed me the freedom to do so.

What is distinct about being a Hindu is a harder question, but it is easier to say how the world perceives us. To an outsider, Hindu and Hinduism is often confused with wearing a turban, free-roaming cows, restrictive dietary choices, vegetarianism, no beef on the menu, the curry, yoga, Ayurveda, idol worship, many gods, caste system, erotic temple sculptures and Utopic monks. That's what the mass media identified us with but not the enchanted visitors to the country. We are much more than how the world identifies us.

We are a people who want our sons and daughters to become physicists or astronauts, not entertainers or cheerleaders. We want them to be thinkers and fair judges, than followers. Not being followers, we are rooted to an eternal belief of "come what may". No wonder we have grown to be different. When I listened to an incident of a packet of curry powder accidentally spilling at an airport customs checkpoint, it might have been a national security concern for the Russian officers, but the intent of the Indian carrying it was modest: He was taking his culture with him on this trip. Likewise, when the young third-generation Indian taxi driver in Durban decided for me where best I could go for dinner, he drove me to a street of Indian restaurants. We always think we have the best.

In fact, we knew the best since ancient times. This made us non-conquerors and non-invaders of any land beyond our geographical territory.[(4)] We took the lead in astronomy, chemistry and medicine.[5] We knew what the "good-life" is all about. I have heard that pluralism, secularism, universalism, acceptance and tolerance, all go along with Hinduism. We knew more about diversity than conformity. We questioned more and answered less.

Hinduism is grossly misunderstood, and Hindus themselves mislead and misuse it. So much so that people hesitate to call themselves Hindu. In fact, many would find it hard to define what being a Hindu means, and if he does attempt it, his definition would greatly differ from another's. The trouble is not with the people. It lies in the formless and structureless nature of the religion itself. Pew Global Research Center in its 2014 report put Hindus just a few points above Muslims in America, in spite of the positive contributions of Hindus there.[5] The religion also hardly gets any significant mention or representation in the world. Often Hinduism does not find significant mention when the West reviews world religion. Many authors make only a passing remark about it in their writings. Hindol Sengupta makes an interesting reference in his book *Being Hindu*, where he says, "Richard Dawkins, perhaps the most well-known gene biologist alive, wrote in his book, *The God's Delusion*, mentioning Hinduism only twice in 460 pages."[6] I see it as a questionable treatment meted to the oldest school of thought, or probably a religion, on Earth.

*

The origin of this so-called religion is thought to be in the region of the Indus Valley Civilization, which now lies in northwest India, a flat, fertile and riverine region. Archaeological excavations have discovered artifacts used by early humans, including stone tools which suggest an extremely early date for human habitation and technology in the Indus Valley. Human habitation in the region has been traced to 60,000 years BCE, and cultivation of cotton around 5500 BCE. While the civilizations of Mesopotamia and Egypt have long been recognized for their celebrated contributions to civilization, India has often been overlooked, especially in the West, though her history and culture give enough evidence of her influence on the world.[7]

History puts it as a consolidation of a set of thoughts and philosophy, later to be known as Hinduism, around 5000 years ago, or even earlier. This is the time when the rest of the human world was probably grappling with basic living. It seems, after reading various texts, that the words Hindu and Hinduism were bestowed on us by outsiders such as the Greeks and Turks, rather than by people who practiced this philosophy. Today, the words have come to loosely represent a certain geography, ethnicity, culture, and a religion.

While doing my research for this book I got an opportunity to visit the city of Madurai in southern India. I had gone there to deliver a series of college lectures on my last published book, on climate change and environment. The trip and the plan were put together by my former university colleague and a good friend, now a professor at the local university. I was going to meet him after many years, so looked forward to the trip eagerly. After the talk, the idea of visiting the town of Rameswaram came up. This town is on the island of Pamban, between India and its neighbor, Sri Lanka. There is a mythical Hindu story attached to a particular place on the way to Rameswaram. All of this filled us with greater zeal and, thus, made the trip much more fulfilling.

The ancient Indian epic *Ramayana*, one of the most important texts in Hindu literature, narrates the story of Rama, prince of Ayodhya. He had won the hand of the beautiful princess, Sita, but was immediately exiled with her and his brother, Lakshmana, for 14 years, as part of a conspiracy hatched by his stepmother. In the forest, Sita was abducted by Ravana, the demon king of Lanka. Rama gathered an army of monkeys and bears to find and retrieve her. Together, they constructed a stone bridge across the sea and attacked Lanka (now Sri Lanka), killed Ravana, and rescued Sita. It is said Rameswaram is the place from where Rama built a bridge across the sea to Lanka. The Ramanathaswamy temple, dedicated to the Hindu god Shiva, is located at the center of the town and is closely associated with Lord Rama. Built between 12th and 16th CE, the bridge is in the state it was when it was made. The temple has famous corridors, which are the longest found in temples in India. The temple, along with the town, is considered to be a holy pilgrimage site for Hindus.

We hired a taxi that took us to the temple and back to Madurai. It was a three-hour trip one way, so we left early in the morning. The unique feature of this island is that it hosts the first and only railway line constructed over sea in India. It's a picturesque setting, where a low 1914 iron bridge ran over the water, almost touching the waves. The bridge also has a mechanism to open for ships to pass whenever needed. Even though there is a recently constructed road link adjacent to it, the place remains protected and the view is breath-taking, particularly when trains pass on it.

This was the second time I would be visiting the island city. The first trip was during my college days, when we visited the place for our "shore collection", an activity that was part of our study trip. We walked the long stretch of the sandy shore and collected various marine organisms. We brought them back to our lab for further study. I vividly recall that trip and was nostalgic about all the fun we had as a group. But this trip was more specific and I intended to visit the temple, which was in itself a sanctum sanctorum for any Hindu. My friend belonged to the inner temple community and was able to quickly put together our plan for a visit. The visit would allow me to get past the long wait in the queue and take me to the innermost parts of the temple, which for some reason remained out of bounds to the general public that came in huge numbers.

We reached the city and were met by our local contact who would guide us to the temple. We were soon in the temple administration office and, after exchanging some pleasantries, were ushered to the temple premises. We took an inner passage cutting through the communal paths straight to the part of the temple that was inaccessible to the general public. I heard the characteristic Vedic chants reminiscent of the bygone days echo within the temple walls. Though I never understood its meaning, it created a deep feeling of numbness inside me. I am not a devout practitioner of the religion and have always avoided temple visits, but in this moment, it played on my senses. A mixture of myth, history, mood, smells of thousands of incense sticks mixed with greasy oil lamps, sandalwood, fresh flowers and the soft sound of hymns overwhelmed me as I stood in front of the deity. I did not hear the priest utter something to me, but a nudge from my friend made me realize he had asked me for my name, place of birth, date of birth and my son's name. I said all of them one at a time and later heard him pronounce them clearly with his chants. We performed a puja, a prayer offering. The priest asked me to make a wish, which I did solemnly: for a safe return. He then presented me with holy water, sweetmeat, flowers and ash. I dropped a small sum in the donation box next to me and walked to the exit. On our way back, I realized how cold my feet had become walking and standing over the moist rocky floor. Later, over a cup of warm tea in the temple office, my friend had said with great conviction: "The Lord will hear all your prayers as he has done to his faithful."

We began our journey back to Madurai that night. The road ran across a vast stretch of open land, dotted with dim, distant isolated villages. Occasionally, we passed a small town with a few shops open, but most of them were shut. I looked through the window at the moonless sky, speckled with stars, and thought it must have been the same always. I thought about the whole exercise and felt in unison with the countless Hindu pilgrims who would have done the same for centuries. Over hundreds of years, people have been flocking to this temple with their offerings and prayers, immersing themselves in the ancient Vedic chants, collecting holy water from the temple tanks, and returning feeling awed. I repeated the feat, not as a devotee of a faith, but as a participant in an act undertaken by millions of people following the same path for centuries. More than the devotion to a deity, the overwhelming feeling of following in the footsteps of millions of pilgrims over a thousand years was a cleanser. It was more of a human path I had traversed that day, which they called a Hindu path.

*

At a glance, Hinduism has become a set of humdrum rituals. A silent prayer, folding of hands, a bow, brief closing of the eyes, uttering a wish, smearing a dot of sacred ash on the forehead, a day of fasting, and numerous shadowy acts set a Hindu apart from the rest. It could sound meaningless, but when this simple faith could bring humans together, it must be more than just what it seems. Believed to be the largest religious gathering on Earth, the Kumbh Mela is held every twelve years in the northern Indian state of Uttar Pradesh. It is believed that 30 million Hindu pilgrims gathered to bathe during the festival in 2013. They have gathered before in similar numbers at the same location but not in such record-breaking numbers as this one. Going by the numbers, it can be inferred that there must be some serious force in this faith.

In nature, animals, too, congregate in large numbers. Millions of insects, red crabs, starlings, wilderbeest, flamingos and sharks come together, driven by the need for food, mates and migration. But a multimillion human gathering at the confluence of three rivers on a specific celestial date and merely driven by a faith defies both natural science and common sense. Why has the event gone on for centuries if the faith hasn't brought prosperity to its faithful? I had asked this question a few times to myself and each time my answer varied. But the only part that never changed was the answer that this event glorified the power of human faith over everything else. A faith driven by a conscious thought, that we have sinned in living our lives and it will be washed away only through penance. It is submission to the earth that they come to acknowledge together.

It is ironic that a Hindu nation never emerged out of the faith which, though, bound millions. Instead, the Hindu land has remained fragmented in large and small kingdoms, along with other charitable states. The territory saw influx of the first foreigners, bringing Muslim ideology from Turkey and later from Central Asia. Buddhism was born in India and spread toward the east. Much later, Sikhism spread to the West. The founders of these two new in-house religions were born in Hindu families. The last inroad into the Hindu land was from the south. In the name of trade, the southern sea attracted ships carrying merchants and Christian missionaries. None of the incoming religions made any dent in the thoughts and beliefs of the Hindus, even after countless atrocities and demolitions being carried out. Rather, these foreign religions remained on the fringes. Finally, a country was mapped out by the last of the colonizers and we had a country called India, where most of the Hindu faithful live today. A secular and democratic country with numerous religions, faiths, intermingled with tribes and ethnic groups. Being the dominant religion, the country has been governed by Hindu prime ministers since its independence. A Hindu wrote the country's national anthem, but surprisingly, the word "God" never occurs in it. Thus, a country of gods had put its land, rivers, mountains, people and diversity ahead of all the gods. The Constitution, which was drafted in the aftermath of Partition and religious riots, gives all its people the right to equality and freedom, right to speak or act against exploitation, right of choosing their religion, as well as cultural and educational rights.(8)

Yet, today, the everyday life of an average Hindu at a glance looks dismal.(9) Hindus see themselves as their own rival, more than anyone else. The daily scramble for life's goodies seems to be everywhere. It seems the religion, rather than unifying and resolving life, has instead shackled them. In fact, the religion hasn't done any wrong, but long ago, the religion was hijacked, twisted and presented to the masses in the form we witness it now. What we see being practiced has the least semblance to what it originally stood for. Castes evolved to enforce order in Hindu society but deprived a section of basic rights. It runs in every home, if not in actions, in words. Today, caste has crept into national politics as a force. The outcome is a complex society which remained divisive, cultivating hatred, living in fear of prosecution, feeling chained. Along with this, there are issues of gender, dowry, social prejudices, unexplained rituals and countless taboos that millions are looking for a way out of. Rather than feeling empowered and liberated by idealistic and free-flowing Hindu thoughts, people go to bed with a troubled mind and walk with hunched backs. Filled with anger and hate, society paints a dismal picture on the whole. Adulterating food, adding harmful dyes to edible goods, coloring vegetables, mass producing fake drugs, exploitation, and corruption in governance, which were forbidden acts in Hinduism, are signature acts of this aggravated society.

I feel now that Hinduism, over time, stands destroyed by countless prejudices resembling plague. These are hidden as infections and contaminants in reservoirs – reservoirs such as the temples of prayer, unhygienic homes, illiterate people and weak and fearful individuals. These weaken the mind and body, disabling rational thoughts. Rather than nurturing human life, society believes in silent broadcast of statutory cautions and uses mythical texts often misinterpreted by leaders to their own gain. Many times, I have witnessed humanity run to temples to seek answers from deities, not knowing the solution lies within them. The result of this experiment, over thousands of years, looks to be a failure.

*

Hinduism is an organic and natural religion. It signifies democracy through its pluralism and tolerance[(10)], and universal truth. It has allowed "cows and Mercedes on the same road with both the owners practicing their rights to showcase their four wheels together". I had said this once to a bunch of overseas visitors, unable to tolerate their continuous caricaturing while on the road. In turn, democracy propagated the idea of selfhood. It sees God in every individual. It pushes all toward self-awareness and consciousness. It is called a religion, as there is no other way to define a mass of people numbering tens of millions believing everything natural as 'Godly'. A river, rock, tree or animal, they can all be held to be sacred. They preach Jesus, Allah, Buddha, Mahavira as their own. They have sheltered persecuted men of other faiths such as Tibetans and Zoroastrians and allowed them freedom. They have accepted political refugees escaping certain death from Sri Lanka, Burma, Afghanistan and Tibet. All this happened as part of an unfathomable philosophy. It puts forth a working philosophy, which embodies humanity and the environment together as one. No wonder every animate and inanimate object on Earth was given a soul. Animals, plants, rocks and stones are given godly status. It has understood the restless human body and mind, and has proposed a way out. It has defined virtues and sins not separate from each other but as part of a whole. Unlike Christianity and Islam, Hindus consider humans as sacred and free of sin at birth. (11) To remain so, humans need to do good deeds. Unlike Christianity, Islam or Buddhism, Hinduism is not a religion which has do's and don'ts. It is for the faithful to decide what is good and what is bad. What works for one and makes one comfortable is considered to be as good as religion for him.

Culture called 'Indian'

Hinduism did not appeal to people beyond Indians, or people of Indian origin. Though evidence of it does exist in some far-flung countries, the numbers do not make any big impression. Whatever had spread, most of it could have happened through Indians traveling to these regions and some isolated visitors who happened to take it along with Buddhism, which traveled far and wide carrying Hindu principles. The reason for its limited acceptance is speculative, but saying that it could be because it was not written down fully, does not follow strict codes and conducts and that whatever was available as text remained secretive possessions of the few priests could be plausible explanation. Also, as the emphasis in Hinduism is on the personal, the private, the idea of conversion or spreading the faith by inducting more followers is not characteristically Hindu way of thinking.(12) The end result: the religion has predominantly come to be recognized as the religion of the Indians.

The landmass of India is unique, too, and in some way it has played a role in keeping the country distinct, geographically. The land was formed as a breakaway from the African continent. The high mountain ranges up north, perennial rivers in the east and west, and the ocean down south made it a distinct territory. The people of this territory were natives of this region, and are now proven to have been genetically same over the past 600 centuries. *American Journal of Human Genetics* in 2011 published a finding by a group of scientists, showing that "for the past 60,000 years, no foreign genes have entered the Indian population".(13) No wonder we Indians stand distinct with our features. In fact, so much is our distinction that while crossing the road in one of the less busy residential suburbs in the USA, my friend had put his hands over my shoulder and jibed, "Let us cross faster, or the approaching cars might speed up seeing two brown skins." It sent both of us into a fit of laughter. We continued with the joke and I remarked why he didn't invent a software which once mounted in the car would enable the car to detect the race of the person crossing the road. This would be the first racial car in the market and would turn him into another of the Valley's growing billionaires!

The incident later made me wonder how we have separated ourselves from other ethnic groups and hold deep-seated, shallow prejudices. It may be natural to sneer at a different race or religion because of competing resources, but acts of side-stepping, practicing exclusion, and even extermination, have made the subject very serious. Countless acts of racial cleansing or genocide have been carried out in the past on all continents by almost every race and ethnic group. We are reminded only of the German-Jew narrative, but nothing has stopped humans from continuing to practice similar acts. The incidents in Cambodia along class lines, over ethnicity in Africa and Eastern Europe, and over religion in India are reminders of our weakness, our vulnerability to divisiveness and aggression.

At a dinner meeting with a group of business associates, among whom one happened to be a commercial pilot with the Philippine Airlines, the subject of "what is being Indian" became the topic of discussion. The location was idyllic, on one of the remotest islands of the Philippines. The island was once ravaged by the notoriously famed typhoon 'Hainan' a few years back. Since the disaster, the place is seeing a boom in business, hence this invitation for me to discuss business possibilities in the area. My associate was accompanied by his wife, who, too, flies with him as a senior stewardess. The group also had a few pilots and lady stewards as friends. The discussion shifted to India as their airlines had recently decided to fly a non-stop flight to Mumbai from Manila. In unison, all the flying staff were grumpy about this decision of the airlines. All of them had previously flown to India on the same airlines, but the operation had been called off. Now, it was to be restarted. I was told that the pilots disliked the overcrowded airports and looming haze. The stewardesses were visibly discomforted by the quality of the passengers they carried. One stewardess clearly mentioned that Indian passengers were "unmanageable". The constant mix-ups between different types of meals, which started from a straight Hindu meal, to vegetarian and non-vegetarian ones, without beef and pork. There are also innumerable requests for change of meal during the flight, often leading to arguments. The commotion at the drink cart carrying alcohol is the other challenge the stewardesses faced. There were many more I had to hear that day – from commotion at the aisle, crowding near the toilet, talking loudly, to absurd requests. Overall, their journey ended with complaints of over-exhaustion and unhappiness. That night, I was caught explaining as much as I knew about my fellow citizens, before calling it a night.

While retiring to my hotel that evening, I thought my hosts hardly knew how sorry I felt for them. Little did they know that I myself had faced similar incidents of unruly flyers while flying home. It made me choose my trip carefully every time. Why we paint such discomfiting picture of ourselves to other ethnic groups is something beyond my comprehension, and control. However, our actions and behaviors have often left me embarrassed. I have flown all over the world, to all continents, but this unique flying experience in certain airline routes is menacing. It happened every time on my flight from Bangkok to Calcutta. This is one route which suits me going home from Manila. I get very good connectivity and spend less time waiting. The Bangkok to Calcutta sector is predominantly used by nationals from India, who are either on holiday or on business trips. The flight rarely has other nationals or native Thailanders. Every time, the flights are full, overloaded, and noisy. The boarding is like a free-for-all. No sequence is followed. Maybe, they abolished it as most people do not read their boarding passes, or are incapable of reading English. They crowd around the gate once the door opens. On this route, we all fly business class! The rest of the trip is what my hosts had narrated to me.

I try to board my flight at the earliest, as, once in, I hardly find place to stuff my hand carry in the upper bin. They are all taken and stuffed to the maximum. Soon after leveling off, the seat belt sign is turned off as per rules. But then, that is when the passengers stand up and block the aisle. They form groups to exchange notes about their creative ventures in the suburbs of Bangkok. I am forced to listen to the lucid narrative, often to a level of irritation. As I pass between the rows of seats toward the exit after landing, the scene of the carnage is noteworthy: garbage, leftover blankets, pillows, discarded papers, food items and plastic wraps are strewn all over the seats and floor. The faces of the lined-up air stewards and stewardesses betray sulking and they often avoid greetings. I try to give them a hearty smile for their patience and for looking after us. I have moved away to another more expensive and time-consuming route since then, but I cannot escape from this messy legacy of being Indian.

Indian travelers may be untidy and careless, but they have a surprising philosophy as to why they are so. When asked casually about the filth all around while disembarking, one said sheepishly: "It's the airlines' job to clean up as we are paying for trip." A simple way out indeed! The result of this attitude has made the government of Mr. Modi to pledge cleanliness as one of the top agendas, under the banner of 'Swachh Bharat', or 'Clean India', putting a stamp on the fact that Indians have dirty habits.

The mess continues elsewhere, too. I recently came across a near hilarious article written by a traveler to India in the national newspaper The Hindu. The author, Evald Flisar, is a celebrated writer and I quote him verbatim here so as not to cut the extent of his troubles with India.(14)

He writes: "Some people say that I am half Indian by now. That may be true, but I still need an Indian visa. It has never been difficult to obtain one, but recently it has turned into a nightmare. To get one from the consular section of the Indian Embassy in Slovenia, you have to turn up in person with a filled-in application form, two square (2x2) recent photographs with a white background, bank statements for the last six months to prove that during your stay in India you can support yourself, with all your fingers intact because you will be finger-printed, a passport of course, and with 193 EURO in cash to pay for the visa (no credit cards!). It is somewhat easier and cheaper to get an e-visa from the comfort of your home, but even there you can only narrowly avoid a fit of rage when you discover that in Slovenia, nobody makes square passport photos with a white background, and that for uploading the photo (once you manage to get one with the help of at least four clever friends) the JPEG has to be more than 10 KB and less than 100 KB, and that a PDF of the passport must not exceed 300 KB or be less than 20 KB.

"And then, the real trouble starts down your road to India. Filling in the application form. They want to know which places you want to visit, and why, which countries you have visited in the last 10 years, and all about your mother, father, wife and employer, education and the sort of work you do or have done in the past, and quite a few things besides, including the address of your stay in India. You may intend to visit seven different places, but under "address in India" the form will allow you to enter only one (for example, Ashok Hotel, New Delhi). You may be retired, but the form insists on entering the name and address of your employer, even their phone number! What to do? There is a list of countries that you may click for place of birth and nationality for yourself, your wife, your father and your mother, but my father and mother were born before the First World War in the Austro-Hungarian Empire, and there is no such country on the list! So, you have to improvise and click Yugoslavia, which also no longer exists, but is at least on the list, and clickable. And then, after giving your credit card details to God knows who, you are promised to receive your e-visa within 72 hours."

*

A bank manager in Taipei had asked me if I was a professor at the local university. I had gone there to undertake a bank-related service. A quick conversation with her revealed she considered Indians as intellectuals and that they primarily work in places such as universities. I was impressed by her disclosure. In Turkey, while flying domestic, the gentleman sitting next to me had inquired if I was in the country for business. We were traveling from Istanbul to Sanliurfa, a city bordering Syria. Only a few foreigners traveled this route after the Arab Spring uprising. The gentleman did business with India and had invited me to his factory on the outskirts of the city. In Kunming, China, they detained me for a special interrogation and full-body and luggage check. At Vancouver airport, the immigration officer had politely ushered me to a waiting translator to further process my papers, not knowing I understood the language well and possessed the skills to fill up the disembarkation form by myself. Traveling Indian Punjabis often seek this help. Countless incidents related to my being an Indian are in my record, but when an opportunity to be a citizen of another country came by, I spontaneously decided: I am not giving any part of my Indianness away.

Being Indian, however, has one incapacitating aspect, and it affects me and my work. Thinking about a travel overseas at short notice is always a time when I am reminded of my nationality. I need a visa for practically all countries on the map. I have had to cancel trips simply because there was not much time to process my visa, which often involves checks and cross-checks, filling up special forms, and lengthy waits. In fact, my passport stays with my travel agent, more than with me. It has now become dog-eared, dirty, colored, stapled and stickered.

I traveled invariably for work, so always had a reason to enter a country. Countries have provided me travel clearances with the paper documentation I provided them. But it was the United States embassy in Manila which required a personal interview. My travel agent was nervous as her clients had been turned down before. In the aftermath of 9/11, visa had been difficult to procure. My agent was with me and carried every document she could gather for me, so as to support my cause. The call to check them finally came and soon I was seated in front of a young lady officer. She looked at my passport and the first question loosened me thoroughly. She asked if I was from Chennai. My passport mentioned my address, while in my first job my permanent address was in Chennai. When I answered in the affirmative, she went on to say she had lived there and was working in the US consulate in Chennai for three years before arriving in the Philippines. She joyfully shared her experience of the food, clothes and culture, which she most enjoyed in Chennai. The travels to the beaches and to the city of Pondicherry down south were her most memorable experiences. The interview turned into a conversation and it was over even before I had realized.

Being Indian can also be a cultural disadvantage. There have been incidents where just being an Indian made a negative impact and denial of facilities. I, too, experienced a few. The first one was after I was invited by the University of Lahore in Pakistan. Later, I had to give it up, because when my travel agent spoke to the Pakistan embassy, she found that it would take months of bureaucratic reasoning to get an approval. Again, when I arrived in Singapore, I learned that people went slow on renting out flats to Indians, specifically to males living alone or in a group. My agent, while telling me to be a bit patient while I was on the lookout for one myself, had remarked: "Indians have often left the place untidy, dirty and damaged." One house owner had found nails driven into the walls, and marks of candle soot. Others found heaps of dirty plastic in the stairwell and another had had his wallpapers destroyed by moist cloth. Hanging household items on walls, burning oil lamps, incense sticks and hanging wet clothes indoors are a way of life for Indians. I feel sorry for their habits. Surprisingly, the occupants in all these situations were well-educated and they had failed to realize the mess they created. This is because, in their respective homes, the perennial culture is that someone else did the chores for them.

*

The daily needs of an average Indian are very less. He is content as long as his philosophy is running. But note, we are also known for our actions. We have conquered space science by regularly sending payloads to orbit using our own rockets. We reached Mars on the lowest possible budget. We are a powerhouse in developing logical software running countless devices and machines. We are masterful traders. We have the finest strikers of the cricket ball, and much more to list. But the very best we have given the world is in meditation training. Known to be one of a kind, the Vipassana meditation course has worldwide following. It helped engineer the mind across cultures, races and among followers of various religions. I had a glimpse of the demand for it when I had often failed to get a desired slot to enroll for one. This is what we should be known for, as our true identity.

Proud being Bengali

In addition to being an Indian Hindu, I am also a Bengali. Sudeep Chakravarti, in his book *The Bengalis – A Portrait of a Community*, sums up: "The Bengalis are the third largest ethno-linguistic group in the world after the Han Chinese and Arabs. In fact, this nomenclature is a celebrated combination."[(15)] He says that this community has "produced legendary political leaders and revolutionaries, iconic movie stars, unending stream of writers, philosophers, painters, poets and musicians". He claims, "Bengalis are among the most civilized and intellectually refined people on earth, but have been also responsible for genocide and racism of the worst kind". He adds, "Bengalis are renowned for liberal attitudes, but also religious fundamentalism. We are argumentative yet meditative, pompous yet grounded, hypocritical yet the wisest among all."

I am a Bengali, a Hindu-Bengali to be more precise. Today, it is estimated there are close to 95 million Hindu-Bengalis spread out around the world. Hindu-Bengalis are a distinct culture, well known across the country, if not the world. We are known for our inclination toward intellect, literature, art, music, cinema, sports, sweets, fish dishes and traveling. We are thinkers. We are full of opinions. We are conservative and love English. We revere a goddess named Durga and every year indulge in festivities related to her with an elaborate ceremony that lasts a week. We are not very well known as business people, traders, or in jobs needing hands-on skills, or even serving in the military, though there are exceptions to this. One can have all this in one experience when one steps into the city of Calcutta. The top shop owners are mostly from the western part of India. The taxi drivers and the daily wage earners are from central India. The office clerks, true to their nature, are Bengalis. Overall, we are generally easy-going and laid-back.

The state of West Bengal, where majority of Hindu-Bengalis live today, is also unique in many other ways. Geographically, it has common land border with Bangladesh, Nepal and Bhutan. The northern part of the state has the snow-capped Himalayan ranges, while its south is washed by the Bay of Bengal. Because of its location, the state uniquely experiences four distinct seasons, which appear in all local poetry and folk songs. The state has remained agrarian since time immemorial and has never been industrialized. A communist ideology runs in the state, though politically the communist party has been dethroned in the recent past. Majority of the people in the state are Hindus, with a large population of Bengali Muslims. The infamous riots in 1947, involving members of these two religions and which killed millions of Bengalis, are a testament to how divisive religion can be. Finally, the Muslim Bengalis got themselves a separate nation, Bangladesh, carved out from the state of Bengal. This left the Hindus in the remaining part, called West Bengal. Today Bangladesh is rated among the poorest economies in the world. The other half, West Bengal, progressed but fell behind the other Indian states and remains among the poorest, too.

*

My search for an identity for myself ended with concluding that I am an Indian, a country which thought it futile to invade another and dared to pass a common law for its citizens. A country where in schools evolution, not creation, is taught as the origin of humans. A country where a mathematician like Ramanujan described his brilliance as an "act of God"[(16)], but the national anthem misses any godly mention. I am a Hindu, a religion which could not change and keep its faithful together. It is a religion which prays equally to Buddha, Jesus and Allah, and is scorned upon as multi-

Godly. I am a Bengali, a culture which reveres knowledge, art, and a goddess. Maybe, I have erred, but I, without a doubt, stand on a foundation of benevolence, seeking a middle path in life. It has profoundly influenced me to live and act fair and live with firmness. It has propelled me to be creative and remain detached from the fruits of success. It has made me an introvert and a thoughtful type, clumsy to some.

8. Taming Mind

The Malady called 'Thinking'

I took Natural Science and Zoology as my subject of study in graduate school. It made me study living organisms, single and multi-celled. Surprisingly, at no stage in the university curriculum did we cover humans. It is perplexing. Are humans not part of zoology? Or are we something superior to animals and have to be studied separately? My fascination for the human species, however, remained. I am intrigued by their behavior and even more by their actions. Today, as a species, humans have defied nature and natural laws. They have created new organisms, transplanted organs, created babies in tubes and gone to the extent of surgically changing their own sex. Humans are the only animals who are capable of self-inflicted infanticide, as well as killing oneself. Everything about this species is bizarre. While every part of the human body works precisely as in any other animal, the human brain seems to be something unique, unlike any other. There is a theory that just to cool the human brain, the entire body shed its hair cover, so that the skin could easily sweat and cool the circulating blood.[(1)] In this way, humans came to stand out among primates and have skin denuded of most of its hair. Whatever hair was left by evolution was taken off by the business of creams and lotions. Fashionable men and women with skin bare of all hair have become a trend, making humans naked as never before, possibly further helping the over-worked brain!

Tending to physical looks may take a small part of a human's lifetime, as I have personally experienced. Only a fraction of my time is spent in grooming activities, even less clothing it. Much of my active life is spent thinking. I have struggled to keep pace with the present and to be with the now. Thoughts shackle me all the time. Like bubbles, they emerge from deep down, come up to the surface and burst, leaving nothing but mixed emotions. Thoughts of past and future, events and encounters, plans and possibilities cloud the present. Over time, I have tried not to indulge in them but they remain a part of me. I assume that if they have so persistently remained a part of me, then it must be natural and should hold some significance. I did some research on this and soon found a study which could solve my dilemma.

Barry Gordon, professor of neurology and cognitive science at the Johns Hopkins University School of Medicine, worked on the subject of human thought and came up with the following analogy. He thinks there is an evolutionary significance to it. He says: "Forgive your mind this minor annoyance because it has worked to save your life – or more accurately, the lives of your ancestors. Most likely, you have not needed to worry whether the rustling in the underbrush is a rabbit or a leopard, or had to identify the best escape route on a walk by the lake, or to wonder whether the funny pattern in the grass is a snake or dead branch. Yet these were life-or-death decisions to our ancestors. Optimal moment-to-moment readiness requires a brain that is working constantly, an effort that takes a great deal of energy. To put this in context, the modern human brain is only 2 percent of our body weight, but it uses 20 percent of our resting energy. Such an energy-hungry brain, one that is constantly seeking clues, connections and mechanisms, is only possible with a mammalian metabolism tuned to a constant high rate."[(2)]

He further says that "constant thinking is what propelled us from being a favorite food on the savanna, and a species that nearly went extinct, to becoming the most accomplished life form on this planet. Even in the modern world, our mind always churns to find hazards and opportunities in the data we derive from our surroundings, somewhat like a search engine server. Our brain goes one step further, however, by also thinking proactively, a task that takes even more mental processing". To stay well "our mind is constantly calculating a 'what if?' scenario. What do I have to do to advance in the workplace or social or financial hierarchy? What is the danger here? The opportunity? For these reasons, we benefit from having a brain that works around the clock, more like a sentry on a watch tower, even if it means dealing with intrusive thoughts from time to time".

I presented the above explanation as it is from the reference because there is no better way to explain it. My mind is working overtime to protect my body from past experiences and is planning for future events. Its intrusive nature hasn't changed much, but the nature of thoughts certainly has. The thoughts are updated to be more meaningful to the surroundings and my present state. Urban, social and competitive living has added newer challenges to my life and the brain is overworking like never before.

There has to be a way to get around the "what if" state of the mind, or I would never be at rest. I have never trained myself to meditate or taken lessons in mind-control exercise. There are mind-training guide books and manuals all over the shelves, but somehow they never attracted me. My constant battle with my thoughts remained, but soon I found myself a solution. I started leaving my thoughts to themselves by letting them arise and die out. I did so because they aren't doing any harm to me by themselves. Thoughts which trigger an action are the only ones I need to monitor. In a way, I used my mind to unmind. I never know if this is a solution that works, but I found it a good respite. I soon found that I could free myself from nagging thoughts in another simple way: by choosing the types of thoughts or selecting what to think. I can use the thoughts and the brain energy to do something creative and worthy. Give the mind a puzzle and make it work it out. Surprisingly, this process made me at peace. It brought focus to my work for the first time. The result surprised me and now I have people asking me constantly as to how I manage so much in such less time.

I soon started creating a wish-list for myself, my mind and the body. My list for myself included the work I needed to complete. For the mind, I chose a list of items it needed to contemplate on to accomplish the work I had chosen for myself. And for the body, the list included things that would ensure its timely nutrition, comfort and protection. Anything outside of this didn't matter much to me anymore. An intrusive thought on an unrelated subject is now a matter of "no importance" to me. I am much more at peace now.

The above experiment is a result of careful observation over time. As I went along, I have noticed every time that I was engaged in something serious, my mind was in total control. The thinking and thoughts were focused on the job at hand. I recall my earliest experience of playing cricket. When I was padded up with bat in hand, waiting for my turn to go and take my stance at the crease, I couldn't think of anything but what the ball and the bowlers were doing that day. How is the field being set and what can I to do dominate the game? My mind and thoughts were working to overcome the challenge. Throughout the play and until the end, nothing engaged my mind but the game. Cuts, bruises, hunger, thirst and common bodily concerns are not registered. I have noticed this calm and alert state of mind on many instances. Engaging the mind or giving the mind a task became my mantra. After all, was this the winning formula I had kept asking myself?

*

In spite of the realization, my mind raced and I struggled to control it. It raced to cope with the competition, fanatically worked to counter domestic upheavals, looked for new opportunities and for the next good idea. For humans, it is true that thinking does not end. Humans live for something more than mere survival. Each individual strives for something more, and his or her thoughts go along in the same direction. This is influenced by culture and environment. For a human population of a few billions on Earth, a million things would symbolize life and living. Life to some could be anything from amassing wealth, power, to fame. For others, it could be thrill, adventure, artistic expressions, or social work. The rest just look for peers to ape, or simply look at their neighbor for inspiration and to contemplate on.

Human lives and their living are fundamentally connected to their environment. The environment brings in multiple sensations. Our five senses constantly evaluate these and record them as good and bad, pleasant and unpleasant, and rate them to further store them in our memory. Thus, our memory is a record of thousands of sounds, tastes, smells, visual and tactile sensations. The sweet, smooth, creamy sensation of a pastry remains in our memory and soon we develop craving for it as for many other such things. Craving leads to the feeling of gratification and pleasure. Gratification would mean fulfillment, satisfaction or enjoyment of some nature. The other is pleasure: a state or feeling of being pleased or gratified. It could include some source of enjoyment, delight, amusement, diversion, worldly pleasure, sensual gratification, indulgence, preference or wish. Unknowingly, we get bound to our desires for fulfillment and it becomes our life.

If gratification and pleasure are what we seek[(3)], I am intrigued why these words are treated as restrictive or forbidden and uttered in whispers. Religion and culture have anyway banished them. These words carry a flavor of negativity with them, as also the word 'fun'. Many, or most, cultures and societies will take it wrongly if someone says "I am having fun" or "I am having a pleasure-filled life". This is ironic when human motive on Earth is clearly to find a way and the means to have fun and pleasure. Somehow, 'fun' and 'pleasure' got wrongly aligned with worldly, transitory, and fleeting things and their pursuit or even utterance needs carefulness.

Plenty of scripts, fables and quotes are centered around explaining how life is to be lived away from mere pleasures. Eastern as well as Western thoughts have united in their pursuit to explain the 'good-life'. The earliest would be the *Shrimad Bhagvad Gita*, written over 5000 years ago by an Indian sage called Vyas. Ch. 5:22 verse of the *Gita* says: "The pleasures that arise from contact with the sense objects, though appearing as enjoyable to worldly-minded people, are verily a source of misery. O son of Kunti, such pleasures have a beginning and an end, and so the wise do not delight in them."[(4)]

Much later, in the West, Plato put forth a similar thought. In his Gorgias, he explains the "good-life", using a debate between Callicles and Socrates.[(5)] It gives an example of two men, each with many jars. One had all his jars filled with wine, honey, and milk. He had acquired them with hard work. His jars are all filled up, so he doesn't pour anything more into them and gives them no further thought. He can relax over them. The other man has the same number of jars, but they are all leaky. He is forced to keep on filling them day and night. If he doesn't do so, he suffers and has no happiness but pain.

Socrates uses the example to convince Callicles that an orderly and disciplined life is better than life spent chasing pleasures. Callicles remains unconvinced and argues that "the man who has filled himself up has no pleasure any more, and experiences neither joy nor pain, that it is then living like an inanimate object. To have a life full of flowing pleasure, it requires leaky jars. Pleasure must flow out of the jars in order for there to be space for more pleasure to flow in". Callicles argues that this endless flow is a good thing as it brings new experiences and gives new purpose to each moment of our lives. However, Socrates argues that the "good-life" is not found in an endless stream of pleasure but in order and harmony.

Examining the above, present day living makes humans match our present state of continually seeking pleasure as a mantra. Life is lived going after instant gratification for deriving pleasure. Humans continuously follow the "pleasure principle", which is the driving force that compels them to gratify all their needs, wants and urges. Not being able to fulfill them makes one anxious and unhappy.

In truth, human goal is relaxation, but the world we have created around us and the grid we have connected to counters relaxation. The system around wants us to handle a leaky jar all the time. I came across an article which says "humans are not made to relax and seeking pleasures is not an illness".(6) *An Introduction to the Principles of Morals and Legislation* is a book by English philosopher and legal theorist Jeremy Bentham. First published in 1789, it is the first major book on the topic, where Bentham developed his "theory of utilitarianism". (6) The book says that every human action is strongly influenced by expectations of pleasure. Making decisions ranging from which products to buy to which job offer to accept requires an estimation of how good (or bad) the likely outcomes will make us feel. Thoughts about the pleasure feelings, without being in the moment of pleasure, shape our decisions. Researcher Talli Sharot in his work took this observation further and revealed that administration of a drug that enhances dopaminergic function (dihydroxy-L-phenylalanine; L-DOPA) during the imaginative construction of positive future life events subsequently enhances the estimates of hedonic pleasure to be derived from these same events. He says in his paper that "when it comes to making more complex, real-life choices, humans are endowed with an ability to mentally simulate possible future scenarios that help us predict the likely emotional outcome of these events". (7)

These researchers have shown that while imagining future events, activity in the heavily dopaminergic innervated striatum tracks the subject's estimates of the expected pleasure to be derived from those events. They reasoned that if dopamine modulates reward prediction, then its increase while imagining future events should impact subjective estimations of future pleasure to be derived from those events. These findings provide the first direct evidence of the role of a natural body chemical, dopamine, in the modulation of subjective hedonic expectations in humans. In short, pleasure is natural and an essential part of human decision-making. The actual pleasure felt from pleasure-ful thoughts shapes many of our decisions. This is how we buy a house even when it does not exist and sign on a life insurance when we are alive.

Psychologist Paul Dolan's work shows that our decision-making mostly has two separate components – a pleasurable component and a meaningful one. The pleasurable part is the instant gratification. The meaningful component is our perception of how purposeful an action is.(8) In the end, it would mean every action requires a decision that is derived out of pleasure. Thus, pleasure is here to stay with humans. This explains why a certain flight journey turns out to be comfortable when you know your girlfriend would come to receive you at the airport.

Mind has Moments of Awakening

I had arrived in Honolulu for an international conference as an invited speaker. It was a prestigious conference and I was among the chosen few to talk. I was given a room on the 29th floor of the Hilton Hotel on the beach front. The front desk had already cautioned me that the room had a breath-taking sea view. Upon checking into the room, I nearly dashed to open the balcony door. What I saw was more than what I had anticipated. The sun was setting below the distant horizon. A spectacular wash of orange and golden glow filled the vast expanse of the sky, forming a perfect backdrop to the blue ocean. I could hear the calls of sea birds hovering in the gusts of sea breeze, which blew against the building wall. I was in a deep state of pleasure as I watched the beautiful canvas from the balcony. It seemed I had connected myself to the earthly Wi-Fi and that too without keying in a password. I stood there long to savour the setting before me. And yet, the mind was working to sum it all up for me. I thought about what had brought me to experience this heavenly moment, the people who had helped me in the background, making this blissful experience possible. Their faces flashed past one by one. I pulled the weather-beaten chair towards the balcony edge and sat down to thank them. That was how my mind responded. It made me wonder how beautiful the mind was, and yet it holds malice.

I recall another instance, when a friend I was visiting at hospital had said: "It is good to be sick." I saw a book near his bed. I had never seen him near a book before and knew he hardly read. I picked up the book, a collection of short stories, and seeing me turn its pages, he said I should read it, too, if I hadn't. "They are very moving tales of people and their lives," he said. He certainly must have been at peace to say that. A person when ill or disabled would temporarily turn to benevolence, a puzzling behavior, because as an able body he was just the opposite: uncompromising, selfish, boastful, demanding, angry or ill-tempered. Explaining a similar scenario, Eckhart Tolle says: "When you are ill, your energy level is at its lowest and the intelligence of the body takes over the remaining energy for the healing of the body and there is not enough left for the mind for egoic thinking and emotions."(9) He explains: "Certain miracle healing and quick recoveries which cannot be explained by medical science get cured in this fashion. People who believe they want to heal and get well put all their limited energy in the body and get out of the disease sooner than the rest. Others who keep diverting their energy to their emotions continue longer with their treatment and at times become chronic sufferers." This is the power of a human mind which awakens to perform a miracle.

Create a Brain to Control Mind

It was discovered that the brains of London's cab drivers, famous for their navigational skills down to knowing the smallest details of the city, were being physically altered by their work. Maguire writes in Proceedings of the National Science Academy: "Structural MRIs of the brains of humans with extensive navigation experience, specifically licensed London taxi drivers, were analyzed and compared with those of control subjects who did not drive taxis."[(10)] It was found that the posterior hippocampi of taxi drivers were significantly larger relative to those of control subjects. A more anterior hippocampal region was larger in control subjects than in taxi drivers. Thus, hippocampal volume correlated with the Black Cab drivers of London who had intense training and learned how to navigate through thousands of places in the city, which takes about two years to acquire on average. The most interesting part of the article is when the authors ask "whether similar environment-related plasticity is possible in other regions of the human brain outside of the hippocampus".

In his book *The Brain That Changes Itself: Stories of Personal Triumph from the Frontiers of Brain Science*, Norman Doidge gives numerous examples of functional shifts in the human brain.[(11)] He narrates an instance where a surgeon in his 50s had suffered a stroke. His left arm was paralyzed. During his rehabilitation, his good arm and hand were immobilized. Slowly, the bad arm remembered how to move. He learned to write and play tennis again. Here, functions of the brain areas killed in the stroke were transferred to healthy regions. It shows that the human brain has the amazing ability to reorganize itself by forming new connections among brain cells. A catchy phrase explaining this neuroplasticity is: "neurons that fire together, wire together", as described by the Hebbian Theory.[(12)] It also shows that when two events (neurons firing) occur in the brain at the same time, the events (neurons) become associated with one another and the neuronal connections (wiring) become stronger.

Changes in the brain in relation to the environment and specialist functions may be natural. Plastic changes occur in brains of musicians, compared to non-musicians. Christian Gaser and Gottfried Schlaug compared professional musicians who practice at least one hour every day to amateur musicians and non-musicians.[(13)] They found that gray matter (cortex) volume was highest in professional musicians, intermediate in amateur musicians and lowest in non-musicians in brain areas involved in playing music: motor regions, anterior superior parietal areas and inferior temporal areas.

Looking at these researches I wonder: Would it be possible for us to make our own brain and finally develop a desired type of mind? Can we bring enduring changes in our brain to control our thinking? I was electrified when I did locate one such report. The work was done by Richard Davidson, a neuroscientist at the University of Wisconsin, and is now well-known. He led an experiment in cooperation with the Dalai Lama on the effects of meditation on the brain. Over the past several years, he had helped recruit Tibetan Buddhist monks for research on the brain and meditation, at the Waisman Laboratory for Brain Imaging and Behavior, University of Wisconsin, Madison. The findings suggest that over the course of meditating for tens of thousands of hours, the structure and function of the brains of long-term practitioners had actually altered. More interesting were the differences between monks and the novices. The monks had much greater activation in brain regions called the right insula and caudate, a network that underlies empathy and maternal love. They also had stronger connections from the frontal regions to the emotion regions, the pathway by which higher thought can control emotions. These results would suggest that long-term or short-term practice of meditation results in different levels of activity in brain regions associated with such qualities as attention, anxiety, depression, fear, anger and the ability of the body to heal itself. Notably, all these functional changes may be caused by changes in the physical structure of the brain.[(14)]

*

It makes sense to me. Now I know why we seek good schools, great teachers, creative careers, nice friends and beautiful environment. I know why we want to be religious and follow religion truly. All of these involve intensity, rigor and discipline, as were needed by the London cabbie and the Buddhist monk. And all these would shape our brain structure so we can think clearly, develop empathy and decide wellness. We raise our children with the best of everything, but today while writing this piece I realize we fail to give them what they need most: inspiration and training. A similar scenario is played out elsewhere, too. We lack motivators, stimulators and visionaries in our society who would churn the masses to think good and live contented.

9. Mastery of Body

Feeling of being 'kidnapped'

The first realization of a body comes from experiencing pleasure, such as while taking a deep breath and inhaling a lungful of air, being fed with good food, taking rest, or being touched, cuddled or hugged. Unlike a bubbling mind, the body is easier to handle because, as Eckhart Tolle puts it, "the body runs by its own intelligence".[(1)] Though this intelligence is universal, bodies are born different in gender, physical looks, abilities and, importantly, the amount of pain inside. Notice how the surrounding environment is influenced by the body characteristics of a newborn. A bouncy and beautiful baby body brings pleasantness, gentleness and happiness, while the reverse brings displeasure, some curse, ill-fate or a thought of bad karma. The gender of the baby is a big defining factor in most cultures around the world. A boy is always the wish and a girl is a consolation in large parts of our society, specifically covering Asia, Middle East and Africa.[(2)] While the East has always focused and looked inside the body for its true identity, Western culture attaches importance to physical appearance.[(3)] And as a Western life style is the preferred way now, the need to 'look good' defines our life and living.

Mocking our inclination toward self-presentation, Hollywood comedian Billy Crystal had famously said: "it is more important to look good than feel good".[(4)] The culture of "to look good" has overwhelmed our mind and entrapped an intelligent body, pushing it to overwork to a level of suffering. As Baumeister and Bushman explain, getting a sun tan, undergoing plastic surgery and taking to smoking or alcohol are proven risks we might take just to look cool.[4]

There might be an evolutionary reason for it, as explained by the authors. They say "we humans achieve all our social goals by being accepted by others, so self-presentation matters".[4] To serve this push towards self-presentation, solutions have come handy to end the wait and suffering of people. It is easy to alter one's physical looks, sculpt a new body shape, rework a face, construct a new nose, tone up the skin, or graft someone's hair, all to better oneself and bring parity. Body enhancement goods and brands are frantically browsed and bought to elevate oneself physically. Those who still fail to look good enough take to built-in software to alter their looks using photo-shopping skills. Social networking sites have come to the rescue, allowing these alterations to be circulated around.

*

I have grown fully aware of my body and looks – a man with average build and physical appearance. I had looked at myself a million times before someone pointed out to me that I was losing hair. From then my perception of myself changed. I started seeing myself as among the bald personalities. I frantically looked for signs of the same in others around me. It was not difficult to find some in my group, but I noticed they had run for cover and resorted to medical procedures to restore their looks and diminishing pride. However, I decided to let my head shine. This form stayed with me. It did not deny me any of my objectives. Rather, I realized it gave me a character. It changed how I thought at times. I would joke that every hair down the drain is a dollar in my bank account, and many more things. I even researched and made a list of famous bald people around the world to show that one is not less a man with a little less hair on the top. The list had sportsmen, artists, literary greats, scientists and even a prince. It was a consolation to me that life could be normal like any other. Yet, the day I was told about my baldness, I identified for the first time with a body form.

Best of all, my body never faced any challenges with the lifestyle I had adopted. I never abused my body and balanced my life well. I quickly rated items and activities which I would never seek beyond my taste or worthiness of the items and activities. Purpose was on top of my agenda. Fun and pleasures were priority but mindfully chosen. I learned to take control of my emotions, so the body enjoyed its freedom of performance all the time – until I committed myself to the institution of marriage. It brought me a partner who was close enough to be me, but not being me. Soon, the partnership ran on open emotions and the body ran paralyzed. The mind and body did not work in tandem, as an external body tried to run me and my body. This is the only time I felt misplaced and 'kidnapped'.

Mine was a perilous state, best explained by what Eckhart Tolle wrote: "In intimate relations, pain-bodies are often clever enough to lie low until you start living together and preferably have signed a contract committing to be with this person for the rest of the life. You don't just marry your partner, you also marry his or her pain-body. It can be a shock when perhaps not long after moving in together or right after a honeymoon, you find suddenly there is a complete personality change in your partner. The person is a total stranger now."(5)

I felt captured and held captive but took to my mind to free myself. I gave it tasks to perform and allowed an unrestricted way. This was an amazing state, where my mind allowed me to roam free, think unlimited and contemplate and plan possibilities, even as the body was being held between do's and don'ts. Thinking of it now, I remember I had compiled a list of literary brilliance undertaken when the body was held under various circumstances but the mind practiced liberty. The best literary work of prose and poetry are examples of this state. *Don Quixote* by Miguel de Cervantes, *De Profundis* by Oscar Wilde, *Hymn to the Pillory* by Daniel Defoe, and *Conversations With Myself*, a collection of Nelson Mandela's writings, were all composed while they were in prison. Sir Walter Raleigh wrote *History of the World* while locked up in the Tower of London for 13 years. The writings of O'Henry were in prison. Fyodor Dostoyevsky's *The House of the Dead* was written while he was serving time in a Serbian labor camp for opposing the autocratic government of Russia. Gandhi spent a lot of time in prison for civil disobedience and did most of his writing while being held there. There are other examples of known and unknown literary achievements in situations where the body was held captive, demonstrating another of the body's masterful acts.

Monogamy a Cultural Thing!

Humans are social animals and not designed to live by oneself. We have developed special cues to pick our group, friends and mates. We become so specialized in our association that we can identify our loved ones from a crowd or can recognize his or her voice among a host of noises and even transport their pain into ours. We just have to be in love to realize this power. The same senses work inside us to protect us and differentiate an intruder or an enemy from the surroundings. However, it is always a challenge for a body when it starts living with another body, while the "love and hate", "friend and intruder" is being sorted. Marriage is one such stage in which one could experience it.

My thought on this subject remained and when opportunity presented itself, I examined it. Once I was home for a long break. This time, I chose to do some reading. I had been buying books, but most of them remained unread and were piling up. While browsing one of them, I did not notice that evening had set in. The intensity of the book's content had kept me going since afternoon. Away from the city, the evening sky had turned dark. I was in my armchair on yet another of my trips to my farmhouse. It was a sultry day. I looked up at the vast canvas of the sky at its natural best, when a fast-moving spec of light streaked past. Satellite debris, I thought. But it took my thoughts to humans and their menacing activities on Earth. During the day, I had met a long-lost school friend and taken him out for lunch, where we exchanged updates. He had inquired about my relationship and marriage. I was probably the last one to have got married among our classmates, who were still in touch. I laughed at his question and quipped, "Marriage is not a natural thing, so I am rightfully going through upheavals." I had expected a spontaneous comforting word or comment from him, but it never came. We were silent for a while, as I was ruminating on what I had just uttered and probably trying to understand what I had meant. Marriage has surprisingly become something which when mentioned elicits more silence, flashbacks, cover-ups, light-hearted jokes and nothing more.

The primeval difference between man and woman presents a challenge to their union. Though the body looks for a union as soon as it reaches maturity, the mind processes the complexities involved. Given free will, very few conscious humans will jump at the idea of getting married and having children. If they do overcome this dissuasion, it would be citing peer pressure, the need for a successor or someone to take care of them, other incentives and some selfish interests. Customs and traditions see to it that these incentives are in place – society's rewards to make people do the near unthinkable. Even States are taking up this subject in recent times, not for love but to populate. Marketing corporations have jumped into the fray in a bigger way. The picture of a blissful couple is used for selling anything from homes to kitchenware. The alarming number of people falling apart or seeking separation is evidence that making good relationships is serious business and involves much more than the mere incentives that everyone promulgates. Expectations of role play often bring man-woman marital relationships to an end. Despite this, the search for a perfect match continues somewhere deep inside everyone.

I have witnessed the burdens that come with marital relationships. I lost some of my friends to it. I had attended marriage ceremonies with a heart filled with best wishes, only to later feel remorse. Attending them, I was witness to two intelligent individuals unwittingly going into oblivion. Once they took their vows, they seemed to be lost. They wouldn't answer calls on time, missed regular gatherings and were not free on weekends. They even changed their choice of colors, favorite restaurants, clubs and temples they usually visited. Some changed jobs and cities. They came to have completely altered personalities. I had dreaded such change in me, but, nevertheless, it caught up with me, too.

The moon now appeared in the sky outshining the stars into obscurity. I could hear the evening shrill of cicadas nearby and howls of jackals in the distance. I closed the book I was reading and my thoughts went back to an article on mate pairing in animals I had read a week before. Zoologically, humans do not fit the faithful, committed, steady definition when it comes to man-woman physical relationship. Writing in the journal Nature, Joe Cormier said: "Obviously in this situation of monogamy, marriage is a limitation in terms of natural selection and evolution of natural human traits. In the natural world, monogamy or "faithfully married" does exist, but very few. In evolutionary terms, monogamy hinders natural selection, a process by which a species improves its chance of survival."(6) Monogamous species include black vultures, hornbills, a species of night monkey, wolves, otters, a few hooved animals, some bats, certain species of fox, and the Eurasian beaver. The most studies have focused on the North American prairie vole, which is a mammal and rodent. They are known to pair for life. Three-quarter of the pairs of this species remains intact until one partner dies. The living partner rarely acquires another mate. Thus, these animals became a subject of interest to neuroscientists and endocrinologists who study social behavior of animals. The article published in the journal Nature finally explained the cause for this intriguing "mating for life" behavior.

Researchers Zuoxin Wang and his colleague in an article in the journal Nature Neuroscience have shown for the first time that the act of mating induces permanent chemical modifications in the chromosomes, affecting the expression of genes that regulate sexual and monogamous behaviour. (7) The researchers found that genes for the vasopressin and oxytocin receptors had been transcribed and as a result the nucleus acumens of the animals bore high levels of these receptors. Animals that had been permitted to mate also had high levels of vasopressin and oxytocin receptors, confirming the link between bond formation and gene activity. Mating activates this brain area, which leads to partner preference and the same change occurring in the brain with this drug is a possibility, the researcher claims. Interestingly, the injection alone cannot induce partner preference. "The drug by itself won't do all these molecular changes – you need the context: it's the drug plus the six hours of cohabitation," says the lead researcher.

This type of behavior has been linked to the hormone vasopressin, which is released when a male mates and cares for the young. Due to this hormone's rewarding effects, the male experiences a positive feeling when it maintains a monogamous relationship. To further test this theory, the receptors that control vasopressin were placed into another species of vole that is promiscuous. After this addition, the originally unfaithful voles became monogamous with their selected partner. These very same receptors can be found in the human brain and have been found to vary at the individual level, which could explain why some human males tend to be more loyal than others, the research proposed. This made me conclude our faithfulness to each other seems to come from both body and mind – the receptors from the body, and the intent and purpose from our mind.

Being Superior in an Inferior Body

While a body cherishes its state, its gender can be a trap. I am born a man in both body and mind. God is a man, too, and on my side in this venture. Growing up, I separated my toys, chose different games, sat in a separate section in class, and learnt to differentiate commodities associated with the two sexes. I chose boys' things all the time and later, men's. Many years later, I decided to buy my first car with an automatic transmission. Cars run on a complicated gear system, which I disliked. For my choice, I was made to wait longer than the rest for my car. The showroom did not have one and had to retrofit my special request elsewhere. When my friends heard about my choice, they asked why I chose a women's car. My decision was natural. I was looking for driving comfort over other features. Today, nearly everyone drives this version of a car.

Perceptions of gender related differences are woven deep into our culture and accepted as a way of life. In the end, women stand on the less privileged side of the gender scale. Luckily, I had a head start over my opposite sex from the beginning! Compared to them, I enjoyed more privileges in most aspects of living. An interesting article, titled 'From Cradle to Cane: The cost of being a Female Consumer', talks about a study of gender pricing in New York City in 2015. It showed that on an average across all chosen categories women's products cost 7 percent more than similar products for men. The items included girls' toys and clothing, adult clothing and personal care products as well as home health care products for seniors. Women paid an annual gender tax of approximately USD 1,351 for the same services as men. Such biases can be found elsewhere too.[(8)]

At the recent Cannes Film Festival, I watched a bunch of women artists standing on the red carpet, seemingly unified and speaking for equality with men at work. For some time now, lady tennis players have been demanding that they be given the same winner's prize as for men. While institutions have recently started admitting women as members into certain 'Men's Only' places, churches have done the same by admitting them as priests and recently the ban on women driving unescorted was lifted in a Gulf nation. Similar equality efforts ring all around. Since when and why women became a "sub species" and under-privileged is an intriguing evolutionary and social question I had asked myself for some time.

Meanwhile, women who have not found what they had always wanted in society have decided to adopt the difficult way to prove they are no less. They have joined the movement to impress men. This has gone to a level where we see them play every game men enjoy playing and watching, including thrashing each other in wrestling matches. Why is there no game which only women play and men try copying? This phenomenon has taken women everywhere now, but not to a place where they matter most: in true partnership with men. They appear, but more as a token. In fiction, they are featured for the charm and to provide the twist. Elsewhere, they appear in books, but the books are titled maliciously. Philosophy skims past them. Religion is ambiguous about their status. Glossy magazines do much better, baring them superficially stopping only at the bottom of their skin layer. This throws up a social question: "What are they, after all?"

As a student of natural science, I am aware of the role a female plays in a species. Growing up from school to college, I saw women mates fall into a stereotype state. Exceptions stood out but were too few to make any mention. When it was announced that we would be flying in an all-female crew plane, many clapped and no one panicked. We took off and landed smoothly as expected to end this intriguing story. Women can do all jobs as men do. However, I found women different from men in many ways, beyond a set job. Despite many years of bondage and subjugation, their inner perception of the world has remained very different from men. This probably comes to them naturally. After all, they are meant for a different role. At times, it makes me feel they may be superior to men. Their different perception of the world obviously creates doubt among men about whether they could be true partners to men and perceive the world as they do. Over time, women have become inferior by the design of human culture. It is a debilitating fact, not conspicuous but widespread, that human culture is skewed toward men. It should lead us to raise questions when we realize that women who make up half of the human population had been kept away in the making of the "human culture". Or, shall we call this culture now a "man culture"?

Author Angela Saini researched and reviewed scientific articles and theories and recently came out with a book titled *Inferior.*[9] I would argue the choice of the title because when I started reading it, it was with a bias and in a more sympathetic mode towards women. However, soon I could see parity and connect with the content correctly. As I read every evidence it presented, I narrated it to my mother, who could only say, "I knew it inside me all the time", without taking her eyes away from the chores she was doing.

The life of a woman begins in the womb very differently from a man's. Researchers have shown that the mother's placenta does more to maintain the pregnancy and increases immunity against infection if the baby is female. No one precisely knows the cause. It could be to balance out the natural sex ratio of more boys to girls in the natural world of humans. This might be nature's way of correcting the balance by giving more chances of survival to the girl. [10] Once born fortified, the girl outlives a boy at all stages of life. Database on human longevity in 38 countries reveals the robustness of a woman's life over a man's.[9] Angela Saini further cites Steven Austad, an expert on ageing, to dismiss the notion that the reason for this could be environmental as the man is more exposed to harshness due to the nature of his work and often indulges himself in unhealthy practices such as smoking and alcohol. Eventually, the longevity is well reflected by the Gerontology Research Group in the US, which confirms that among all the super-centenarians, only two are men and 46 were women. Biologically, they outlived men far and clear, thus establishing their biological dominance.[10]

Longevity is the cornerstone of a body's success in the natural world and women have taken the lead in this aspect, compared with men. They have lived alongside men since the beginning. They have functioned as part of a group, the smallest of which is the family. The environment they have faced and the food they consume are the same as men. They worked side by side with men while starting and raising families. These thoughts came over me as I watched the Asian Games in Indonesia, where athletes of both sexes participated in their respective disciplines. I witnessed a female athlete who ran her steps with grace and dispatched the javelin. I could only say she could be a fearsome hunter if taken back to prehistoric times. Women graciously threw, shot, jumped, ran endurance races and played in group games with acumen as ace athletes. Their body is capable of feats for any type of living, such as using tools to hunt, running, jumping over obstacles, and devising strategies in a group. And it is rightly so, as written in *Woman the Gatherer*, by Adrienne Zihlman. She concluded that "women made and used tools to obtain food for themselves and their children, walked long distances, carried food and infants bipedally in the evolutionary past".[11] This epitomizes a woman's physical capacity. We, however, do not know about how prehistoric social structure functioned and how men and women functionally lived. What made women secondary, a receiver, a property, and pushed them to the fringes of humanity in general could at best be a wild guess.

One does not have to look far to see a prehistoric woman and to feel nostalgic about the existence of an equal culture. My lady office manager is nothing less than the picture of that prehistoric woman. She worked tirelessly and when she became pregnant, her first, I was expecting she would take a long break from work. Astonishingly, she worked without a break. She ran her house, cooked, washed and commuted to work, until she delivered the baby. That too came on a weekend, when she sent me a text message saying she had delivered a baby girl and was looking to be away from work for some time. I had replied, "You are not away, but very much at work!" Amazingly, she was back at work in a month. From a toddler, her baby girl has now grown up to be a school-going kid nurtured by a vivacious human female being, her mother.

*

The great plains of Africa, where we evolved from our forebears, is a place of female power. Spending a few days at one of the national parks, I had become aware of their brute resolution to take their species ahead. From the ever-alert elephant matriarch leading her herd to pastures across our tour path, the alpha female hyena leading a team across the plains on a hunt, to a lioness mindfully devising her strategy with her sisters for a wilderbeest hunt are a picture of synchronicity towards success. Child care, running a family, and survival are the success that has been female-centric throughout the animal world. Males worked mostly on the fringes and brought in strength, security and vital support. His investment of his time and attention is well rewarded by the females, who nurture his genes in her offspring.

Female-centric human societies had existed before and exist now. The female in these societies takes centerstage and it is not much different from the natural world. There exist human matriarchal and matrilineal societies where females dominate inheritance and running of the family. These have existed in societies which are ancient, such as in China, India and Africa. In Yunnan, located in south-west China, an ancient Tibetan Buddhist community lives with their grandmothers at the helm of things.[(12)] Her sons and daughters live with her, along with the children of those daughters, following the maternal bloodline. Men live on the fringes, often or not involved in the upbringing of the children. Men and women practice what is known as a "walking marriage" – a sort of hook-up. These range from one-night stands to regular encounters that deepen into exclusive life-long partnerships, which may or may not end in pregnancy. But couples never live together. "For Mosuo women, such is often a pleasurable digression from the drudgery of everyday life, as well as a potential sperm donor," says Choo Waihong.[12]

There exist a number of societies in north-eastern India, southern India and other parts of Asia and Africa where women dominance is acceptable form of family structure. These are standalone examples of womanhood and women's capability in raising a complete family by herself as in the natural world. These must be the very few cultures remaining where the human female is at the helm. But the news is these societies are breaking down and degenerating into the obvious stereotypes. The conformity to the surrounding has unmatched incentive. What intrigues me is: when in our history of evolution did we take control over the woman form and make human culture look what it looks like now?

We have often run to remote societies, which live in seclusion, to gather information about us. I did the same, searching for scientific reviews to see if our societies were skewed toward males right at the start and if yes, why. I came across this interesting article written by William Buckner, a student of Evolutionary Anthropology at the University of California. He writes: "In the realm of reproductive success, hunter-gatherers are even more unequal than modern industrialized populations, exhibiting what is called "greater reproductive skew," with males having significantly larger variance in reproductive success than females. This means we were male dominant from the start."[13]

He writes further that "according to some anthropologists, nomadic forager data suggest a human liking toward equality, including gender equality, in ethos and action, yet the available data does not support this notion in the slightest. On the contrary, in 1978 Robert Tonkinson found that among the Mardu hunter-gatherers of Australia, Mardu men accord themselves greater ritual responsibility, higher status, more power, and more rights than women. It is a society in which male interests generally prevail when rights are contested and in the centrally important arena of religious life. Among the

Hiwi of Venezuela, and the Ache of Paraguay, female infants and children are disproportionately victims of infanticide, neglect and child homicide. It is quite common in hunter-gatherer societies that are at war or heavily reliant on male hunting for subsistence for female infants to be habitually neglected or killed. In 1931, Knud Rasmussen recorded that among the Netsilik Inuit, who were almost wholly reliant on male hunting and fishing, out of 96 births from parents he interviewed, 38 girls were killed (nearly 40 percent)."(13) Females seemed unwanted across many societies.

Despite the strength of the female body, they have submitted to men in mainstream living. Over time, men have taken charge, often through desperate means, and designed the system to fit them. Women show their reluctance to fit in, but those who give way are generously rewarded. The field of science serves as a fitting example. Winning Nobel prizes may be used as a passing measure of this and is frequently used by authors. Since 1901, there have been 825 male winners of the Nobel Prize, but just 47 female winners. Of these, 16 have been for peace and 14 for literature. This signifies a massive gender disparity in contribution to science and society. There could be many reasons for this disparity and the best could be that there are too few women working in frontier areas of research. Or it could be gender bias, as in the case of Rosalind Franklin.(14)

Psychologist Corinne Moss-Racusin at Yale University did an interesting experiment, in which over a hundred scientists were asked to review a resume submitted by an applicant for the vacancy of lab manager. Every resume which was passed on to the evaluators was identical, except that half were given under female names and the other half under male names. The evaluators rated those with female names significantly lower in competence and hiring ability. They were also less willing to mentor them, and offered far lower starting salary. Surprisingly, the sex of the evaluating scientists did not change the bias towards the candidate. This proved a clear prejudice existing in the culture of science, also showing that women are themselves discriminating against other women. [15] Over the years, the culture of science chose a gender bias, leaving women virtually invisible in laboratories across the world. This could be happening elsewhere, too.

It seems everything was against the female gender, which pushed them to the fringes. The combination of strength, competition, division of labor, child-bearing, or mate guarding played a role. But it is clear now that the male dominance over the female is purely a cultural expression, invented and acquired universally by societies all over the world. Humans invented a way of life which subdues the rightful woman's way. Further cultural conditioning through behaviors, such as sex being made off-limits, adoption of celibacy as a means to remain religiously cleansed, calling free and independent women witches, enforcing restrictions on abortion, veiling women under customs and restricting free availability of contraception are classic examples that moved women's wishes to the sidelines. In hiding, they lost their biological strength and turned into a form of cultural commodity. Such is the shortfall that an appointment of one of a them as CEO, head, leader or to any top position makes headline news, and a statistic.

As Richard E. Leakey and Roger Lewin wrote, "There are many formidable and deeply entrenched barriers in the way of women who wish to participate equally in the political and economic life of our society which are all constructed on a basis of social prejudices and conditioning. These remain intractable because of long evolutionary history which planted a propensity of sexual differentiation with males as dominant status."[16] Trying to break this will be surely reciprocated, as Angela Saini gave evidence of. She wrote: "In Norway, since 2006, the law has required that at least 40 percent of all listed company board members are women. Yet, a report published in journal Social Science and Medicine in 2016 reveals that Nordic countries, which have rated year after year as the happiest countries in the world, have a disproportionately high rate of intimate partner violence against women. This could be a backlash effect as traditional ideas of manhood and womanhood are being challenged."[(17)]

*

No one is a winner in this body war. Deep inside, we will remain fascinated by each other's capacity and role. Ancient Indian scriptures had tried to get over this duality by putting forth a line of merging thoughts and creating a being called "Ardhanarishwara", a half man and half woman form. There are many interpretations of this form, but the one I chose here, Ardhanarishvara, "reconciles and harmonizes the two conflicting ways of life: the spiritual way of the ascetic as represented by Shiva (the man), and the materialistic way of the householder as symbolized by Parvati (the woman), whose purpose in Hindu mythology is to lure the ascetic Shiva into marriage and the wider circle of worldly affairs".[(18)] I felt this interpretation closest to being a truth.

"Is Sex Dirty? Only when it's being done right"

"Is sex dirty? Only when it's being done right." I remember reading this Woody Allen quote.[(19)] The moment I read it, I felt his wittiness at work. A fair subject matter, but which remains under a cloak and dagger. Societies have avoided talking about it, philosophers have skirted it, the celibates do not know how to enforce it, and educationists are confused how to present it. The worst of all are the religions, which considered sex as sinful and unnatural; or else why were Gods, Goddesses and their messengers born of virgins? But it exists in all bodies and minds in all its trueness.

I watched sex and waited for every moment to watch it more. Being a zoologist, I had my laboratory full of organisms. From plants, to insects and micro-organisms, they were subject matters of my study. I needed them to court, mate and multiply in large numbers so I could conduct my tests on them. I introduced males to suitable cages where females were housed, provided them food, water and perching places and privacy to make them feel at home. I watched them court, mate and reproduce with their own kind. Microbes, grasshoppers, moths, beetles, frogs, rats, rabbits and guinea pigs mated in my laboratory. The chemicals everyone uses at home and in one's bodies go through countless screening tests on these godforsaken creatures before they hit the stores. This is life with sex to me.

I recall once a friend was visiting me in my lab. He was a mathematician and he could not fathom what I was doing with all the living things around. His math did not work in my lab. Suddenly, one and one did not add up to make two in my lab; it made more. He felt as if he had walked into another planet. True to his profession, he was looking at the logic around me, and I was trying to explain my logic to him. I recall explaining to him that what he did with numbers, I did with organisms. I could see the look of confusion on his face. He didn't seem to understand sex. Maybe, he never wanted to know it, as the culture around him forbade him to do so.

I write my thoughts as the news of the Pope visiting Ireland is played on television. I see him crouched over a piece of paper and reading out to an unexpectedly poor turnout of assembled faithful. With shame, he regretfully asked for forgiveness for the church's ill-treatment of young and adolescent children. Over a period of a few hundred years, the Catholic church has sexually abused youngsters in a way which could be punishable in any civil society. This also comes amid intense pressure on the Catholic church, following a grand jury report in Pennsylvania that found that a few hundred clergy members throughout the state had been accused of sexually abusing more than 1,000 children, for nearly a century.[(20)] Other parts of the world, too, have witnessed similar uproar in recent times against religious guardians. People on the street and in the news scream about what went wrong. I believe, in this case the body's natural urge took over the culture of the church.

Hindu mythology of saints in deep penance and dancing girls trying to distract them has been depicted in many places. This is a message that sex is a powerful force, second only to gravity on Earth. Sex is in progress all the time around us, but we seem to remain ignorant about it. From calls of birds perched on the window ledge, the bloom of garden flowers, to a poached egg and a glass of milk on the breakfast table may sound like a description of an idyllic vacation, but I say they are all sex items. They are produced for a complex process of biological reproduction. While to the rest of the organisms it comes naturally, for humans it is often laced with hush, rules, rituals, or silence.

It takes a huge amount of energy to win a mate in the natural world. It takes even more to make it romantic. I am reminded of my study of spider mating behavior in graduate school. The female ate her mate while he attempted to mate, or was in the act of mating. Many spider species as well as a few insects go through this act, unknown to the theorist. Thankfully, humans have devised working methods to simplify this conquest to a great degree of success. I recall episodes from Indian epics, where kings arranged contests to test the bravery, strength and mastery of a suitor to lure the best men to marry their daughters. The tradition remains in practice among all classes of Indian society, but without the physical conquest. Sunday newspapers continue to post soul seekers in marked categories for ease. What is contested now is the weight of the candidate's curriculum vitae.

Over time, traditions have changed, with more chances for man and woman to meet. From a chance meeting at a club, to over the near-free internet, there are many solutions to resolve this natural urge socially. The other day I was reading in a local daily a small snippet of a young college-bound man who threw himself in front of a speeding train and killed himself. The police revealed he had posted on his social media page a day before that he had been rejected by the lady he was pursuing. Rejection can take any shape in humans, and often dangerous, such as in the form of revenge.

This rejection has turned into a social behaviour; one such is "sexual harassment", which is making news headlines now.

*

I was in the waiting area of the Bangkok airport, changing flights, when I saw a bunch of young monks in their monastic attire and backpacks. They were accompanied by a senior master. The young monks were frolicking and laughing. It seemed this could be the first time they would fly out to somewhere. Their master was serious and looked grumpy. The young were a noisy lot and were busy taking pictures, moving and adjusting so that all of them were equally covered in the camera frame. They just looked like normal kids to me. I thought how their life would turn out as they grew up. The one thought which I could not escape was that they would commit to celibacy, to pledge their legion to the monastery. I am aware there are ways to adopt a life of celibacy. Humans are the only beings who can resist and defy nature, and yet remain natural. But what I wondered that day was: Is their master capable of imparting his will to his pupils correctly? Will he help them in their journey of this body-defining transition?

Energy for sex is just an energy. Yuval Harari gives a good example of this energy, quoting a Freudian argument that "armies across the world harness the sex drive to fuel military aggression. Armies recruit young men just when their sexual drive is at its peak. The army limits the soldier's opportunities of actually having sex and releasing all the pressure, which accumulates inside them and redirects its release towards military aggression".(21) This strategy has been used elsewhere, too, such as in sports, when male players are kept away from their female mates on match days. Further, I came across an interesting observation by Desmond Morris in his book *The Human Zoo*, where he wrote that "individuals with vast lust for power suffered from physical sexual abnormalities".(22) He gave two examples where an autopsy of Hitler had revealed that he had only one testicle, and the same on Napoleon, that he had "atrophied proportions" of his genitals. He wrote further that both had unusual sex lives; it's a guess how Europe would have looked if they were normal individuals.

Take away the energy, and sex is listless.[(23)] The man scaling a mountain, or on the start block of a race, or engrossed in a game, watching a movie or composing a poem has his energy elsewhere. Sex is out of the blocks for him. Ram Das, a Californian practitioner of the teachings of the *Bhagavad Gita*, writes lucidly in his book *Paths to God* that there are stages in his 'sadhana', or work ritual, when the amount of energy he has within him is very important. He says "Hinduism is not the only tradition that teaches this. Even Saint Augustine had prayed: Lord, give me chastity and continence – but not yet."

In the book, Ram Das narrates his experience handling his energies: "When I was doing very intense hatha yoga and pranayama practices, where the breath would stop for long periods of time and the energy would travel up the spine, I was using all the energy I could get my hands on. But the passions are always lurking! Even though I was eating pure, light and living in a very unsexy environment in a temple in India, still, every now and then the sexual juices would flow. This deeply affected my yogic practices."[(23)]

Sex, like breathing, hunger, sleep and creativity, is a powerful drive built into us. It is one area where the body rules over the mind. It's primordial and natural and we can't treat it lightly. Ram Das, however, clears the air by saying: "Each one of us has to deal with the different levels of our energy and with different level of attachments, so what is right for one person is absolutely wrong for another."

Dodging around Dead Bodies

Humans love their lives and search for ways to extend it the most. Such is their love for themselves that they wish to live as dead, too. A trip to England took me to a place where

Shakespeare remain buried. It is in a Church of the Holy Trinity, in Avon. The last months of his life were difficult times as I read through his displayed biography next to his grave. Also were the words, "Death is the gateway to eternal life." The words piece together our zeal for life, even in death.

It was the death of a close friend and business partner that once brought me to the cemetery, which was desolate, except for the few of us. I stood among the head stones thinking. The occasion threw a challenging feeling inside me. On the one hand, I was saddened to see a friend my age lying in a coffin; on the other, I was looking at the state of peace he had brought inside him. In his mind, he had planned to expand his business, talked of getting himself a new office and also a new relationship. His mind wanted to live, but the body gave away. Death brought his mind and body together to a state of rest. I did not show remorse but reconciled to the fact that it happened a bit too early.

While the burial ceremony went on, I walked a few paces away and past the tombstones to read a few names. Almost all of them had died at a mature age, well past their sixties and seventies. Soon it will be All Saints Day and this place will be filled with both grieving and rejoicing people. On this day, tens and thousands of Filipinos march to graveyards to visit their dead relatives, near and dear. It is the single largest migration of people in this country in a span of few days. Cities empty out as people drive and commute to their native places across the country using whatever means they find handy. Planes, boats and buses are overloaded with commuting people. The annual ritual chokes up roads, tarmacs and sea lanes. Cities and municipalities often lose control of the traffic and people management activities keep city officials on their toes. It's a spectacle and another example how faith moves humans. At the end of the day, most people are weary to tell me what the real purpose of doing this was. Those who have the greatest number of dead often complain of their misfortune for having such an exhaustive workload.

I am writing about this unpleasant subject simply because I have unknowingly nurtured a fascination for the subject of death. As a zoologist, I have seen cells under a microscope and animals in experimental cages die. I discard the dead and replace them with new ones to continue my experiment. In my lab, while looking for new bioactive compounds against germs, death is the most desired outcome. Death is celebrated and it is eventful in my lab. It symbolizes success and opens business opportunities for me, without me realizing that I am treading on a taboo subject. Taboo or not, our lives are unmindfully motivated by death all the time. Many of our activities while living are influenced by death. We are all preparing for death but without recognizing it. We buy insurance, accumulate savings, invest in properties, have children, in preparation that soon we will be dead. Ironically, we still treat the subject of death as a taboo.

*

Human death is, however, a subject of debate. Religion, philosophy and societies have made it more distant from humans, though it is one's sure destiny and which needs no prediction. A positive event remains shrouded in negativity. A commoner recognizes death as a biological death, a clinical situation where the body ceases to function. Many societies overcome biological death by keeping their dead alive through rituals. Collectively, these actions have led to the suggestion that social death may not happen until someone is completely forgotten, thus prolonging the life of the dead. In a bizarre incident reported in a local daily in India, a man had kept his wife 'alive' for six months on her Facebook page after killing her.[24] I found many more similar reports while Googling this subject. The offender delayed his arrest by keeping the victim alive socially. So are many others who continue to operate their departed loved one's social media account, in spite of their announced death. I guess if this phenomenon becomes popular, 'death' will no longer happen. A weird situation it would be.

On the ground, the scenario was much different. To extend the social life of the dead, ancients in many regions mummified their dead. I have been to one such unique burial ground in the mountains of the Philippines, where the dead are mummified using tobacco, herbs, smoke and fire in an unclosed wooden coffin, and hung on the cliff side. These are the native Igorots, an indigenous tribe living in Sagada, Luzon Island. The practice can be dated back to before Christianity. Their dead are at times left in inaccessible caves. The reasons for doing this could be speculative, but it is thought to be to keep the bodies away from predatory animals, head-hunters or from any other disturbances. Modernity has caught up to this ritual. I hear one can now cryopreserve a body in supercool state, showing our craving for our body has not diminished a bit.

Obviously, the ancients could not comprehend death as we do today through cumulative understanding. An unplanned adventure had once taken me to a very ancient burial site located in south-eastern Turkey. It was a chance visit, as I was in the region on work. We decided to drive to this unique desolate location after the day's work. Göbekli Tepe is an archaeological site in the Anatolia region of Turkey, approximately 12 kilometers northeast of the city of Sanliurfa. The site, consisting of giant 'T' shaped stones with animal carvings and organized in circular patterns, was on a plateau. The historical significance of this place is that each item constructed dated back to over 9000 to 11,000 years. This discovery resulted in the rewriting of human history, as until then it was not known that humans lived in organized hunter-gatherer groups with enough sophistication to create and construct stone artifacts. Though only a fraction of the area is now excavated, the place recently revealed the presence of a new form of Neolithic skull cult.[25] I explored the place and stayed there until sundown to come to terms with the period I was witnessing. This would be the earliest human record of death with a ritual.

I had the opposite feeling when I visited the Taj Mahal in Agra. The monument is also a place of the dead, but celebrates love. Love personified to such greatness that today a world-famous mausoleum stands over the dead. I had taken a road trip to visit a long-lost friend in Brindawan. Agra was on our way and I decided to visit the Taj Mahal. This was not my first time but was happening after a long gap, so I was obviously eager. The place's surrounding had changed drastically, with more crowded shops and built-up construction. However, when I stepped into the compound past the massive gates, the scene was majestic. An icon with its distinctive architecture and a copy. Look at it from any angle, it imposes itself with the same poise. I walked to the underground chamber, said to be the final resting place of Queen Mumtaz Mahal and her husband, Shah Jahan. Both lay side by side, as they might have wished. Later, walking around the marble-stone structure, I could only be in awe. It took the king 22 years to build the world's greatest monument to its finality. I sat in a corner shade and watched people of all ages, men and women, walk past. Some frolicking, others grave. I wondered, a so-called egotistical human who finally fell in love and promised devotion so much so that he took his affection to the level of immortality. This was the story I was told.

Loved ones may keep their dead alive in any fashion they can, but some win over death by being victims of an act. One such memorial site for victims I visited was on my trip to Krakow in Poland. I could not escape the idea of spending a day at the Nazi concentration camp of Auschwitz and Birkenau. Along with me, there was a large group of student visitors from a school in Israel. They had guides who spoke in Hebrew and recited the events as they walked across the vast compound. They placed flowers at points to honor the dead. I walked behind them, trying to catch the solemnness.

The whole place was beyond comprehension. It had served as a prison and was later converted into an extermination camp. Between June 1941 and January 1945, about one million men, women and children perished here. I walked along with the tourist group to all the sections of this infamous place. The sections with heaps of collected human hair, shoes and personal effects were most moving. Children's inscription on wooden sleeping quarters, the dreaded bathrooms, gas chambers and the mass cremation chambers were reminiscent of unfathomable human hate. Historically, genocide has taken place elsewhere, too – in Africa and Australia against native inhabitants. But the scale at which it took place in Nazi-occupied Germany was unimaginable. As I walked out following the rail tracks which had once brought the prisoners in considerable number, I felt a faint smell of human flesh. I knew I was imagining it all from the overwhelming tale of history and the surrounding.

*

The human body is an intelligent system, made to survive to its best. However, death is inevitable and it happens. Culturally and socially, people recognize it as an end and prepare a send-off. How humans treat their dead is a fascinating subject by itself. Shrouded in faith and belief, we continue to follow tradition with our departed. Even the most agnostic gets a respectful send-off in keeping with the faith he was born into. Tradition, which evolved out of our fear and unwillingness to accept death, is used to send us away. In general, Western culture takes death negatively, as a defeat or surrender, and they mourn privately. While in the East, death is more open. I say this as I have witnessed a few myself. But the most bizarre of all was when I saw death being celebrated openly. It was my first time and it happened in Madras. I saw the dead being carried on the road for cremation with a band playing a popular number and men and women dancing around it, hugging and laughing. It was shocking, but I saw this many time again during my stay.

Later, I had the courage to ask people around of this puzzling behavior. The reason given was sensible to me: "He is lucky to escape the perils of living on Earth and now he travels to another world for a good life. His life, as any life, remains precious and is influenced by his immediate surrounding which made him suffer and unhappy. In death, he has a new environment where he can get what he wished for. Undoubtedly, this calls for celebration".

There is a saying, "Die before you die". It reminds me of a National Geographic feature covering a lion tribe. The king once realized he was old, made way for a young male to take over his pride, and walked away to be found dead after a few months. The television crew had been following this majestic beast over years and they grieved at the very site of his final fall to the ground. His self-imposed exile and retreat to oblivion brought him victory over death. He made way, so he won. Other animals, too, do the same, retreating to a quiet place and allowing nature to take its course. It hints that there is only one way to win over death, and it is by accepting it as the end and letting all around accept it, too.

10. Choose Purpose over Happiness

The World is Designed for Depression, not Happiness

We have designed for ourselves a world in which we live but have ceased to understand it anymore.[1] We have taken the membership of a culture, puzzlingly called "modernity" and where consumption of goods and use of services is the cornerstone of living. Our lives have also been transformed from enjoying the act of living, to enjoying the experiences from living. We have shifted the basics of living and have twisted it as an action-filled experience. Food is compared more for taste and presentation, rather than nutrition. Living is compared more to the location and space, rather than safety or comfort. Dress is worn for style and shape, rather than for protection or etiquette. In addition, we also seek competition, a chase, superiority and dominance as life experiences in all our living spheres. We unmindfully pursue them to seek happiness and to quell the fear of missing out.

I was at Istanbul airport when I heard the news of Michael Jackson's death. It was on television all over the waiting lobby. People stood grim, viewing the breaking news. I, too, joined them to catch up. He was a cultural icon and a household name across the globe, but his life was riddled with controversy. His achievements never brought him peace and, eventually, the drug administered to him by his personal physician, intended to put him to sleep, took his life. No one would know what took him to this state, except he himself. His mind-body conflict turned fatal, even though he possessed the power, influence and accumulated material wealth to outlast generations. I remember I had gone immediately to the music store in the airport and bought a few of his popular records in stock. The store had increased the price in an instant to cope with the demand, but I paid without a flinch to pay tribute to a master, a specialist, a creator, a leader.

Even more shocking was the suicide of famed Hollywood comedian Robin Williams, whose career I had followed on screen. When the news of his death broke, I thought it would be an accident. The actor who made us all laugh and smile with his characteristic light-hearted comedy and jokes was overwhelmed by depression and paranoia. He received countless awards throughout his career. But I had read that to remain on top of his stand-up comedy shows, he was put under immense pressure. Once accused of copying jokes of other comedians, he worked, according to his biographer, "an intense, utterly manic style of stand-up, which sometimes defies analysis, at times going beyond energetic, beyond frenetic, and sometimes dangerous, because of what it said about the creator's own mental state". Eventually, his own skill led him to his death.

There are countless examples of such depressing acts around. But one notable act which I cannot escape without mentioning comes from another industry, not the glamorous world of entertainment. It is the life of astronaut Buzz Aldrin. A man who got the opportunity to train for and land on the lunar surface, only the second one, right behind Neil Armstrong. One who took a one-of-a-kind journey, witnessed Earth as nobody else would. A philosophical or a spiritual journey, I thought for him, but he turned to alcoholism and depression following this historic act. Only he knows the real cause for it, as he went past a remarkable twist in life, of being thrice divorced and becoming a Cadillac car salesman in Beverly Hills.

Depression, either medically categorized or the mere feeling of being depressed, is common.[2] How and why it appears and disappears is often baffling. I got curious about this subject of depression of well-known personalities around us. It interested me since, as commoners, we tend to ape them and their lives without knowing they are sufferers, and often of the worst kind. To my astonishment, the list is endless, as summarized by Matt Haig in his book *Reasons to Stay Alive*. He cites names such as Jim Carrey, Alastair Campbell, Angelina Jolie, Al Pacino, Princess Diana, Brooke Shields, Ben Stiller, Catherine Zeta-Jones, Winston Churchill, Abraham Lincoln, Isaac Newton, among others. It made me wonder about the working of our mind.[3]

Depression can happen to anyone. The reason could be anything – from failure, to becoming a specialist of any type, losing oneself to competition, lack of attention, over-estimating life's goodies, to the eventual failure in fulfilling expectations. One reason which surfaces most is the regret over missing out on material wealth. This is the most common parameter while measuring human happiness across different types of literature. It's relatively quantifiable, hence its popularity. We are born in a world that is stocked up with products. These products, from objects to services, are countless and they surround us. As Matt Haig says, "this world is increasingly designed to depress us. Happiness isn't very good for the economy. If we were happy with what we have, the need for more does not arise. The economy stalls and there is less money to be made".[4] To get over this, manufacturers pipe worries such as ageing, insecurity, diseases and accidents, to countless homes. They also channel fun ways to get over boredom by selling vacations, trips and dine-out packages. This unsettling creation often makes individuals seek happiness and contentment from the surrounding world. This is indeed overwhelming, and failure to become part of the trend often sends an unwary one into an automatic depressive mode.

Interestingly, the conclusion from all this, as put forth by Yuval Harari in his book *Sapiens*, is: "Happiness does not depend on objective conditions of either wealth, health or even community. Rather, it is dependent on the correlation between objective conditions and subjective expectations." Happiness is dynamic, as surroundings change and along with it the expectation, which balloons to a new level. Modernity, which brought in advertisement and mass media, is one sure way to see to it that new objectives are continuously invented and fulfillment of expectations remains distant. This is the design of our world now.[(5)]

Happiest People are in Happy Places

It is beyond conclusion that happy places will produce happy people. But when I read a news clip in the New York Times that a town which is dark, cold and lacked parking is claiming to be the happiest place, I was intrigued. The Finnish town of Kauniainen claims to be the happiest place on the planet. People here are described as melancholic and introverted but are the happiest.[(6)] This is juxtaposed against a perfect sun-bathed island, which most would think to be the happiest.

Reports have suggested that the "chance for humans to become happy is driven by strong economic growth, healthy life expectancy, quality social relationship, generosity, trust and freedom to live the life one wishes to live".[(7)] In an extensive review article in National Geographic, author Dan Buettner rightly points out that "these are complicated entwining factors often linked to the state or country one lives in".[(7)] He eventually concludes that the happiest people are in the happiest places. Happy places are generally happy countries. I was looking through the recent edition of *World Happiness Report 2017*, edited jointly by John Helliwell, Richard Layard and Jeffrey Sachsat John. Their list bunched Norway, Denmark, Iceland and Switzerland as the top four countries, followed by Finland, the Netherlands, Canada, New Zealand, Australia and Sweden. All the top four countries rank highly in all the main factors found to support happiness, such as caring, freedom, generosity, honesty, health, income and good governance, according to the authors. What was notable was that many South American countries featured in the top 25, such as Costa Rica, Chile, Brazil and Mexico, over countries like the economic powerhouse, Singapore.[8] The ranking order has not changed much in the 2019 report.

It would, however, be a mistake to conclude that the countries featured on the top of the list provide some type of happiness package. Making it to one of these destinations and happiness would engulf one is not the case. It never works that way. A country can only provide higher chances for happiness. A country is, after all, in a transient state. It can change. It can even vanish from the map altogether. Status and stories of countries have changed drastically over the last few decades, so has their demography. The story of the USA and California is one glaring example where living standard has changed in the last 200 years since gold was first discovered. Bestselling author Thomas Friedman and co-author Michael Mandelbaum in their book *That used to be US* gave a glimpse of what went wrong with America. [9] In one of their sections, titled 'California here we come', they write: "We cite California's present condition because it is an all-too plausible forerunner of America's future. Once upon a time, both United States of America and the state of California were the envy of the world. Each was favored by geography, natural resources, leading to development of institutions and customs that made it a prosperous, creative, exciting place. Each became a fast-growing place for opportunities and people flocked in millions. The American public-private formula for prosperity – education, infrastructure, immigration, research and development, and the business-friendly climate reached its zenith in California. It had seemed the legend that "American streets are paved in gold" had come nearly true.

The authors paint a thoroughly changed scenario as they write: "In the first decade of the 21st century, the state was facing unemployment rate of 12.5%. Its fiscal condition was dire with state budget deficit exceeding $25 billion. The state's basic failure, however, has been a political one. The only people who are doing well in the state seemed to be the firefighters who earn a salary of around USD 144,000 per year, compared to an average annual wage of USD 52,000." The authors say that "while California's population has continued to grow, approaching 40 million, more people now choose to leave the state each year. If the state has not died, the California dream is now on life support".

Today, the best of American thoughts, theories and values are found elsewhere. The documentary '*Where to Invade Next*', by Michael Moore in 2015, was an eye-opener to me. I watched it a few times just to get a complete grasp of the subject. Moore points out that many ideas such as the constitutional ban on cruel and unusual punishment, abolition of the death penalty, the struggle for the eight-hour day and the May Day holiday, the Equal Rights movement for women, and prosecution for financial fraud during the savings and loan crisis actually originated in the USA and is now in practice in countries like Italy, France, Finland, Slovenia, Germany, Portugal, Norway, Tunisia, and Iceland, but not in the USA.(10)

True, the USA is a story of reduced happiness. In 2007, it ranked third among the OECD countries; in 2016, it fell to 19th. The reasons are declining social support, increased substance abuse, addictions and increased corruption.(11) With declining standards of governance and highest ever polarization with both people and policy, the country paints a bleak picture of a strife-ridden land. The place of China, another economic powerhouse, in the happiness list is interesting. It, too, featured poorly and its general happiness was nothing different from what it was 25 years back. The primary cause was attributed to unemployment and the weakening social safety nets. Many of these happiness determinants depended strongly on social features such as income, healthy life expectancy, having someone to count on in times of trouble, generosity, freedom, and trust. The latter parameters were measured by the absence of corruption in business and government, as pointed out in the report.[11]

Out of obvious curiosity, I checked the ranking of India, the country of my birth. True to my feeling, it did not score any good in the list of countries. We are not a happy country, though we possess all the tools to be one. Humans belonging to older countries, nations with a long history, tend to have stronger pain bodies and, consequently, are unhappier.[12] Further, Eckhart Tolle says: "The state of pain body originates from collective emotional pain people in their region carry with them. This could be from violence, wars, general subjugation, countless prejudices, religion restrictions, unbalanced economics and many more." Giving examples, he says countries like Canada, Australia and Switzerland tend to have lighter collective pain bodies as they have kept themselves out of the surrounding political madness. Whereas, regions such as the Middle East and North Africa, Latin America and the Caribbean have more unequally distributed happiness, reflected by the acute collective pain body.

Certain human races or groups, irrespective of where they live, also face pain bodies of a different nature. Tolle explains that the Jews, African Americans, Native Americans or Australian Aborigines, among other countless tribes around the world, have historically faced prejudices and persecution. Wherever they go and rehabilitate, they will continue to carry an underlying pain body which will keep them away from a euphoric and contented feeling.[12]

The list of places I posted above are, in a way, measures of relative happiness. A comparative happiness index, listing where one has a better chance to be happier. Interestingly, top-of-the-list countries, even though happiest, are surprisingly the countries crippled by misery from mental illness, compared to low-ranking ones. As Yuval Hariri points out, "In Peru, Philippines and Ghana – developing countries with poverty and political instability, fewer than 5 people in 100,000 commit suicide each year. In rich countries and peaceful countries such as Switzerland, France, Japan and New Zealand more than 10 people per 100,000 take their own lives in the same period. In South Korea, which transformed from traditional country to a growing economic powerhouse, the rate of suicide jumped from 9 per 100,000 to 36 per 100,000, from 1985 to date."[13]

People's tendency to be suicidal eventually has no relationship with the happiness of a country. Richard J. Dawson and Brianna S. Schuyler, writing in the *World Happiness Report 2017*, Chapter 5: Neuroscience of Happiness, come out with the best conclusion on research in brain science and happiness. They identify four aspects that account for happiness: sustained positive emotion, recovery of negative emotion (resilience), empathy, altruism and pro-social behavior, and lastly mindfulness.[14] They conclude that the brain's elasticity indicates that one can change one's sense of happiness and life satisfaction (separate but overlapping positive consequences) levels by experiencing and practicing mindfulness, kindness, and generosity. A happy place is any place where environment is flexible and the realist view is taught and practiced. It need not be a country or a town, it could be within oneself.

Happiness is only a Mindset

In Mumbai, on a business trip, I had asked a young street shoe polisher what would make him happy if his wish be granted by chance. My shoes were dirty with overnight dirt from walking the pavement and so did not match the essence of my morning meeting that day. The boy was just outside the hotel gate on the sidewalk along with a few others. He was dark-skinned, with sharp facial features, curly hair and large eyes, features with which he could have passed off as a prince of an estate if only he were elsewhere. It was his appearance that had made me ask this question. He continued to polish and without looking at me said: "I wish more people come this way every day so my business would be good." I gave him a bigger denomination than he would have ever received, and moved away. I could not believe what he had said. The boy had shocked me with his meagre wish. Like him, humans remain focused on their nearest motives and spend their lives improving only those. Achieving these makes them happiest and unmindful of the rest around.

Pursuit of happiness never left me as I grew up. Soon, I realized it remains elusive when I chased it. Surprisingly, I didn't find it in individuals, places, positions, pay packages, travels, objects, or in people's kudos. It lay elsewhere. It reminds me of an anecdote I had read. Alexander the Conqueror, while on his path toward the East, came across a naked fakir sitting and preaching under a roofless shelter. Curious, Alexander asked him what he was trying to achieve, to which the fakir replied: "I am trying to seek nothingness." In turn, he asked back what Alexander was up to, to which he replied: "I am on my way to conquer the world."[15] Both looked at each other. What each thought about the other remains a mystery, and is for us to speculate. My take from this incident is that there are many ways to happiness or contentment. However, looking for a state of permanence in them is a task of the mind; neither material possession, nor material rejection will help achieve it.

We often confer happiness to our feeling of elation, exultation, ecstasy and highs, forgetting that these are orgasmic states which last a few countable moments. What follows is nothing but misery, guilt or simply delusion. I understood that happiness does not lie in living just these moments but in preparing for these moments and the moments after. I found it in the wholeness of living. Living life within my limits was the trick. I discovered happiness in overcoming problems and coming out with a solution. Resolving an issue, challenging myself, or simply accepting a situation. I also found happiness in minimizing anger and irritation. Both come naturally to me, but I discovered that they come to protect me, to inform me of a need for correction. They dissipate as soon as they come, once I take over.

I had prepared my life and work with the same philosophy. Our pursuit of contentment should not stop, even if we do not get accolades. The lack of an audience should not stop us from playing our music, if one is a true musician. Life to me is passing time in truthful involvement, filling up the seconds with activity, mindfully. I found it in simple daily tasks. Cooking a meal is one such act, which I take the most pleasure in. I think about the nutrition, the flavors, the textures and wholeness of the dish for my body. The mind here gets involved in serving the body and in turn makes me happy. The exercise is wholesome. Many such tasks involving challenge, experience, exploration, devising, or planning can lead to contentment. This state is derived from the actual tasks, not from the result. The magical effect all these had on me in the end was that it engaged my time, which is often the cause of all the human anxiety and unhappiness.

I kept my challenges simple and within my limits from the start. Why choose something which is impossible and feel unhappy about not getting it? One at a time, I achieved my set targets and soon a time came when I achieved them all, and more. For me, these were milestones. When I passed them, I often thought what each of them did to me. I realized it made me happy, but I realized it did much more than that. It took me to a state where I felt awareness. Milestones took me to a level where it set me free. It numbed the sensation. It made me inanimate, like a stone. I lost the use of measure, a way to compare, a standard to pitch against. In this state, happiness loses its definition. It is a state of eternal bliss, realization and awareness. It is consciousness. No wonder great achievers have turned to philosophy with ease, while, on the other hand, philosophers transcend happiness.

In a way, knowingly or unknowingly, happiness has become the most sought-after item for humans. Not many, however, know what happiness means, but still seek it to avoid the feeling of being low and depressed. The times one hits those lows are miserable moments. I have experienced them at times. I was listening to author Khushwant Singh talk to

Karan Thapar in a televised interview, where he admitted that he had faced times when he felt low, as if he had wasted his life. Then he looks at his works, the list of over eighty books and articles he had contributed, and his feeling changes. A sense of contentment and happiness soothes him. This is the trick that purpose plays on individuals. It gives a sense of movement, surge, climb, or simply progress, and eventually a sense of happiness. A businessman has his vision for the next company, a politician for his next promotion, a musician for his next composition, a player for the next win, and so the list of purpose goes on.

Mindful involvement in work and toward achievement is a good way to happiness. However, any pursuit of achievement should not be in the hope that happiness would come. If it does, it will be fleeting. The materialistic pathway toward happiness has failed. The idea of having more is somehow unsustainable and never-ending, leaving the individual in a kind of delusion. Also, having less is frustrating, worrisome, not fashionable, thus inviting depression and misery. In his book *The Art of the Good Life*, Rolf Dobelli quotes a famous study conducted in the late 1970s, where researchers analyzed the life satisfaction of lottery winners. The results were astounding, as the winners, after a few months, were found not significantly happier than before. He also revealed that life satisfaction has remained stable, even if living standards have doubled in 18 countries across the world.[16] In another study, it was shown that even though Singaporeans produce per capita USD 56,000 worth of goods and services a year, compared to USD 14,000 for Costa Ricans, Costa Ricans outrank Singaporeans in life satisfaction.[17]

Happiness is just a mindset. It can be achieved by anyone anywhere, irrespective of country, economy, education and benefits. I remember a famed professor of mine who often mentioned to us while at university that he would sit down and write down all his knowledge and experience in a book to benefit students. He kept saying this plan until his seventies and continued to into his eighties. He, in fact, never wrote that book before he passed away. The trick that this imaginary book played on him was it kept him content and happy. It kept him happy thinking of the imaginary book, happy in the imaginary state. Quite possibly, he fooled himself to remain happy.

Irrespective of the situation, the way out from lack of fulfillment is to find a "positive illusion" as a way to deflect depression. I do this often by looking for "positives in the failure" or satisfying myself by saying "there must be a reason why I could not get the deal". Then, as time passes, I tend to find many positives which I gained by not getting the deal. Using these positives, I turn the loss into a good. This is a type of reverse construction by linking all positive events which occurred independently into one, just after the incident of a failure. Missing a flight can be turned into a positive with a call from the school that I need to attend to a child's injury in a football game. Loss of a contract could be turned into a positive as it allows one to have more family time. People who fail to twist their mind similarly are the ones who suffer. It is surprising, and now established, that people who fall into serious depression are much truer to themselves than normal people. Studies have shown that they do not distort things very much, they are willing to take blame, or credit. They are pretty accurate in estimations and also in judging who likes and who doesn't, compared to normal people.(18) In fact, their tendency to understand the reality and the actual situation is high. Eventually, unlike normal people, these people fail to put a positive spin on their life events, which sends them into medical depression. Beating depression and having the feeling of happiness is just a thing in the mind, as the Buddha says: "The mind is everything. What you think, you become."(19)

Happiness Lies in Simple Life-Work

I usually take my winter time off for a sort of self-imposed vacation, which I spend in my farm on the outskirts of Calcutta. The farm is in a rural area among a community that grows rice, vegetables and fish. There are potters and weavers, but they are on the decline. Ancillary activities surrounding farming, however, still persist, from tilling to harvesting. Most activities remain fundamental. Farm products, once harvested, are carried to the village markets and to the nearby town for selling. This has been their way of life since I have known it. It is back-breaking laborious work and in the absence of an industry or other sources of income, this is the only option for the community. Lately, however, the situation has changed. Notably, the youngsters are shying away from the farm and are looking for paid jobs in cities across the country. Signs of prosperity are visible as their income trickles into the community. The changes are visible, such as better housing, television, clothing, motor vehicles and, obviously, mobile phones.

The community has built a small economy and the surrounding world has been observing this transformation. Gradually, I noticed hand-pulled carts advance to motorized rickshaws mounted with loudspeakers entering the area and blaring pre-recorded advertising messages of daily commodities, health products, clothing, movie releases, tickets for shows, medical services, admission to English medium schools, and even new religious gurus who need more members. This is how the modern economy works. Practically, all communities and social systems around the world have been sucked into a globalized culture, which we have gleefully accepted. This is a way of life and the "good-life" seems to be dependent on material gains, nothing less. It finds its way into households across the world and divides them into "haves" and "have nots". This is the beginning of a never-ending race, a cycle of misery, depression and sadness, as I analyzed talking to them over a period of time. Suddenly, a self-sufficient agrarian community had discovered insufficiency in them and their pursuit toward fulfillment is driving them toward unhappiness.

The most happy people we find today live on Facebook. The pleasure-filled acts, the smile on the face have all made this social media platform a place to take shelter when everything around seems to be crumbling. True or not, humans seek happiness and pursue it all the time. It's a state when one fulfills one's expectations, and craving is satisfied. Humans have linked happiness to pleasure and all their activities and efforts are directed toward deriving pleasure to achieve happiness.[20] A route to pleasure that humans mastered long back is the use of intoxicants, and its use has increased many fold in recent times. In fact, so much is the demand that sophisticated science is getting involved in the business of it. Brain-enhancing drugs are being studied and 'Brain Viagra' might soon be available for consumers to reinvigorate mental activity. A recent book, *The Road to Happiness* [21], for example, predicts that the universal use of electrical brain stimulation will allow "direct access to intensive pleasure" bypassing all available stimulants.

Worth pondering is the argument of Frank MacAndrew in The Guardian: "Perpetual bliss would completely undermine our will to accomplish anything at all – that's why perfect contentment has probably been evolved out of us."[22] In his article titled 'Don't try to be happy. We're programmed to be dissatisfied', he asks, "Why, even after thousands of studies and hundreds of books having been published with the goal of increasing wellbeing and helping people lead more satisfying lives, we weren't happier? Why have self-reported measures of happiness remained stagnant for over 40 years?" He uses a survey report presented by NORC at the University of Chicago to make his point.[23]

In fact, it is from author Wayne Allen that the state of the human is clearest. In his book *This Endless Moment*, he says: "Our natural state is not happiness. Our natural state is awake, aware, and feeling our feelings in their fullness. To be at this state, it requires the willingness to feel everything, at maximum intensity."[24] In a way, the pursuit of happiness is futile. But let us not give up our pursuit to earn happiness, as there are ways to be truly happy, too. However, let us be aware that there is surprisingly little scientific research that has focused on the question of how happiness can be increased, and sustained.[25] Drawing on past well-being literature, it has been proposed that a person's chronic happiness level is governed by three major factors: a genetically determined set point for happiness, happiness-relevant circumstantial factors, and happiness-relevant activities and practices. They gave 50 percent to genetics, 10 percent to external events and 40 percent to activities. The authors then considered adaptation and dynamic processes to show why the activity category offered the best opportunities for sustainable happiness.[25]

*

On one of my trips to the outskirts of New York, I happened to notice a group of people quite oddly dressed. They stood out in the crowd of people around the area. They looked like they had walked out of a 19th century movie. The men were in long coats, hats, and were bearded. Ladies wore long skirts and blouses with frills, characteristic of those times. I first thought they were from a theater group and then I felt more convinced that they might be representing a religion or a local cult. In fact, later, I found out that they belonged to a community called the Amish. A community living in parts of the United States and Canada and following a traditional Christian church which dictates all aspects of their day-to-day living, including prohibitions or limitations on the use of power-line electricity, television, telephones and automobiles, as well as regulations on clothing. The Amish value rural life, manual labor, and humility, all under the auspices of living what they interpret to be God's word. This group, by sheer will power, has resisted the global culture. They marry in their own community and continue to have six to seven children. Between 1992 and 2017, the Amish population increased by 149 percent, a figure not recorded in any society in modern history.[26]

My interest to know more about this unique community led me to a book written by Serena Miller, titled *More Than Happy: The Wisdom of Amish Parenting*. She found Amish children to be "obedient, content and remarkably happy", and the reason was solely the way these children were brought up holding on to certain values.[27] She explains that "simple life cues, just like in the good old days, seemed to work in their communities. We, too, knew those cues but have chosen to surrender or give up. Amish children are brought up in a large and extended family, which teaches them to hone their individual skills of managing a broad network of people. This is an attitude that teaches kids to live without shame by being aware of the self, more than the surrounding hands-on skills, and which helps build perseverance, attention to detail and confidence that can help them succeed in any other part of life. They are taught to practice forgiveness by understanding that "making a mistake is not the end of the world", and to use their own creativity to amuse themselves to avoid boredom".

*

Amish life gives us a practicable formula which I came across in my search for happiness. Withdrawing membership from the modern world is one good way to open a path toward happiness. It is true modernity has sent us into depressive state. But why blame modernity? In fact, modernity has also opened countless routes to happiness. It has laid more choices in front of us than ever before. Though the drive to attain material wealth and physical pleasure remain a predominant activity for the masses as a way to happiness, a growing list of individuals are giving up their fortune and future to take to alternative living, new careers, and expressing alternative behavior to seek happiness. Choosing to travel in car pools, living in communes, in remoteness, living as a virtual being, expressing homosexual preferences, taking multiple life partners, accepting a pet as family, using crypto-currency, and thinking of life on another planet are a growing trend. Modernity provides such possibilities and opportunities with reversibility, a point toward an easier way to happiness.

It reminds me of a powerful picture that recently surfaced, of a near naked Sentinelese tribesman in the Andamans island of India pointing his arrow toward the Indian coastguard helicopter when it hovered above to check on them after the devastating Indian Ocean tsunami. The message from the picture is simple: "Leave us alone", even as the rest of the world held up "Help" banners after the natural disaster. This picture shows that individuals or communities can be happy if they set a boundary to their desires and guard it mindfully. Modernity is never a stumbling block in this.

*

11. End of Tussle

Throwing away the Old Ways

How humans should spend their time on Earth is a constant question raised by tribes, organized communities and societies since time immemorial. Cultures and religions took shape, aimed to be a guiding force. What is good and what is bad was identified. The result, however, is often confusing, untranslated and disjointed. Interpretation is often left to the seeker. Looking for a singular answer results in disappointment. Still, we go on our own paths to discover them and believe that we will find one. But soon we find there is something better. People change lifestyle, religion, practices, methods, gurus, but the answer they seek remains elusive. The complexity arises because the "good-life" is transient. Moreover, no two lives are the same and no two lives perceive a thought similarly. In short, collective agreement on what is "good-life" is hard to come by. As Ralf Dobeli puts it: "We are always searching for a single principle, a single tenet, a single rule. The holy grail of the good life doesn't exist."(1)

My search for a "good-life" began with trying to find relief from countless internal conflicts. To start off, many internal conflicts in humans are of animal origin. It originates from lack of fulfillment of all or some of the basic needs. Outside our so-called civilized self, we are thorough animal in every way. An animal is constantly grappling for its survival, food, shelter, comfort, and mate. We are no different. We seek the same path from the very start. The above needs have eventually yielded an order in our society, which has taken a shape and has been etched in stone as "life", or "modern life". It seems that in the end, the more and the faster we can gather life goodies, the better our lives will be. This seems to be the mantra of a "good-life". Sieved through schools, juggling jobs, choosing a place to live in, and choosing a mate thus consume the best part of a human life. The rest is spent in self-improvement and building a status, which Desmond Morris meaningfully termed as "higher motives", in his book *The Naked Ape*.(2)

The principal objective for an animal in nature is to grapple for survival. A fawn takes to running hours after birth; many other animals have also devised their own survival tricks. But for humans, basic challenges of survival have almost been taken care. We are born or give birth under supervision and protection. Our life expectancy has also risen many folds in one century. Naturally, we should be rejoicing, but, ironically, this lengthy aliveness has turned back onto us as another form of struggle. Holed up in urbanity, we are caught up in misery and delusion. Humans who live thus are no different from zoo animals.(3) Zoo keepers have understood this aspect to some extent. So, they provide the captive animals with alternatives. Cages have been replaced by parks and habitats. Some advanced zoos have added recreation and playtime for the animals to avoid boredom. We never know if we have indeed solved their needs by doing so. In the wild, the same animals would be jostling for basics and their time spent in their struggle to survive. The one surviving longest could be the one enjoying the "good-life".

Instead, human living has moved away from a mere struggle for survival to what one does for a living in a short span. A century ago, most of our ancestors would have competed with nature to stay safe and alive. "Good-life" was a life which successfully overcame the natural odds and survived the longest. It was organic. It was how nature defined the fittest. Today, as their descendants, we compete not with nature, but to stay over other competing humans, a neighbor in most cases. The one who goes ahead in this race is termed the fittest.

Modernity and modern living has generated plenty of time for humans. Rightly, we are killed by boredom and the new challenge is the struggle to keep oneself entertained. Consequently, television and social media feeds have taken over a good part of our lives. Undulating drama, negative news, challenge shows, sports and rivalries are choreographed and watched to seek pleasure. Shopping has become another of our favorite pastimes and goods have become essential mediators in maintaining all forms of relationships, and also identity. A solemn day such as the Memorial Day in the USA has turned out to be a day of sale(4), so too have similar occasions elsewhere. All of these fuels a feeling of euphoria. They work as drugs and hallucinogens. The amazing glueyness of the electronic feeds and the loads of advertisement are influencing our behavior and human thought process. These are creating new cultures and, in turn, defining a new generation with a new type of "good-life". In quick time, the new development has changed us and our perspective of living. Unfortunately, all forms of material possessions, from an Island home to looking good, did nothing to relieve our discomfort. Somehow, the feeling of misery inside remains, in spite of all the excess.

*

Every newborn who comes into the world already carries an emotional pain body. As Eckhart Tolle writes, "Babies having heavy or dense pain body cry a lot to draw attention in a way making everyone around unhappy as they are themselves, and often, they succeed in doing so. These babies come into this world with a heavy share of human pain. As the baby's physical body grows, so does the pain body." However, he says that "people with heavy pain body have better chance of spiritual awakening. Their pain body drives them to a place where they cannot live further and this in turn serves as the motivation to an awakening".[(5)]

Many of us hit this motivational spot in our lives, with or without deep-seated pain. At times, circumstances and situations turn us toward it. But the best is when the awakening comes impulsively, or naturally. I had asked people whom I knew well about their orientation toward their internal conflict and how they dealt with it. Their revelation fascinated me. Irrespective of their country, religion and economic status, each had devised his or her own form of inspirational method. I would say some of them were crude. Isolation from the grid, simplified living, eating organic, running out from the city often and taking on a guru are unpolished methods. They can, in fact, add to further identification problems and added bitterness. One may soon find out that one is not isolated enough, simple enough, or organic enough and that the guru has a questionable character. The cycle of conflict will emerge again.

While religion, or faith, has not appealed to most humans in a way so as to define the elusive awakened state, or "good-life", and how they should spend their time, commercial interests have achieved this more successfully. Companies have provided gateways to fulfill human motives. Pick up a magazine in a waiting lobby, or log into any social media, you will notice the thousands of stimulating advertisements informing individuals how they are missing the fun, and thus "good-life". Commercial advertisement through television, print and social media has overpowered the human thinking process and successfully dictated actions. In another way, these have taken over the precious time humans have on earth and turned it into their business. Today, companies boldly claim to be the premier "way of life" brands in the world to attract sales. Virgin Group, one of the world's largest hospitality groups, has coined a caption: "Our products are all about enjoying life to the full, by offering customers excellent value for money in so many areas of their lives. We aim to make them happier."[(6)] I wish a similar slogan is found written on school campuses and in temples of faith, where it matters most.

I lived most of my life like a "jumping monkey", between an intelligent body and a wavering mind. I suffered from something of a "what next" or "what more syndrome". I didn't know what I was looking for and what would culminate into the eternal objective inside me. The world around kept raising the bar for me to leap higher and jump further. It did not allow me to realize when I had hit my optimum capacity. We notice this state elsewhere, too. Artists, writers, musicians and inventors are mostly known by their masterpiece or creation in the form of a single song or painting or an invention. The South Korean pop artist Psy, unknown to many, sang a single dance song and became a worldwide hit. From presidents to the Pope, all danced to its tune. He tried a repeat of the formula with a million combination of tunes, but nothing clicked as that single chartbusting number. We want to break into the charts every time and live to make it our life mission. This turns a specialist life into a continuous chase.

I realized getting out from a chase is the beginning of the path toward recovery and toward a right way. Humans have one life to live, but if one feels he or she is pained by the current one, then it is time to give it away and get a new one, so he can be in the right path. The physically challenged have retrofitted themselves and climbed mountains. Tycoons have become monks and monks have left their congregation for family life. My salvation, too, lies in realization of my inner urge, and in following it.

Salvation in Freedom

My tussle and final objective was to get freedom as a way to "good-life". It started long ago, even before I realized it working deep inside me. But when I realized it, I took all efforts to seek it. Early on, there was a choice to work for a company in the West or move to the East to start a venture with uncertainty. I chose the latter. I am not sure what induced me to turn down a fixed salary job then. But today, I realize I had looked for freedom unconsciously. Freedom is sought by everyone subconsciously, little knowing what their bondages really are. A friend once, over a cup of coffee, talked about gaining freedom from all the nonsensical things around her. I had suggested then, "Just think you are free, and you will be so. Nothing shackles you except your own self. I have tried it on myself and it's working." But if she wished to experience a bit of it, as a start, I had suggested she shut her communication, social networking and see how it felt. She did it on my advice and, in a few weeks, came calling, surprisingly depressed. It seems nobody had looked for her and cared to drop by her office or home to check if she was fine. She felt she was not cared for and all the people around were selfish, and she went on talking about them, in anger, disgust and dismay. I clearly remember saying to her in the end: "At least this much free you are, which you had never realized."

We humans, as individuals, are unrestricted, disposable, replaceable and unwanted most of our lives. We only attach ourselves to our surrounding, to people and the system. This inner knowledge of our own worthlessness makes us worry and feel insecure. The fear of being left out drives us to these attachments. Most of us turn toward being copycats, without realizing that by doing this we are sacrificing our freedom. This takes us on a path of comparison and competition. We ape an idol, copy a neighbor, outdo a friend. People even change family, friends, companion, place, profession, ideology, a nose, and even gender to free themselves, but unknowingly they get bound to the pursuit of this new idea of freedom. The cycle turns over again, keeping one in shackles and away from being free.

What is it then to be really free and to set oneself on the path of attaining freedom? I was aware, however, that the word freedom could also spell doom. Use it at home, office and in public and I may get more attention than I ever got. The same word stands for defiance, dislike, disobedience, discontent, and more. Nonetheless, I looked for it every time and in every place. At the start, I didn't not know what I was looking to be free from, but to be free always gave me a hint of a good feeling, a "good-life". Growing up, passing childhood, through adolescence and into adulthood, the definition of freedom changed from one to another. In childhood, it was escape from the monotony of school and the compliances. It quickly shifted to multiple subjects such as freedom from body, beliefs, culture, emotions and such. Freedom was also to get away from the stiffening orderliness and an organized system. I felt every time, and in every place, someone seemed to know better than me. There appeared to be a "big brother" watching and controlling me. But as I took control of myself, I soon realized that this big brother was full of double standards. One is treated differently from another. What works for me does not apply to others. The big brother chants exotic hymns but speaks ill to a seeker at his door step. He punishes for silly violation but lets one go once enticed. He promises quality but adulterates the goods. He cheats to gain from his followers. I rebelled inside not to follow any. I wanted to shout aloud at the stupidity around and move away to liberate myself. The idea to get away from the muddle grew stronger, not knowing it followed me wherever I went.

In spite of this, I had a deep feeling that "good-life" can only be achieved through freedom. Growing up, I naively thought I could achieve it if I could live a life of 'The Hardy Boys' or swing free in the African forest like Tarzan. I also thought I could become a steam engine locomotive driver, a sleuth, a cricketer, or a comic strip creator. Innocently, I thought the skills would take me to freedom. I didn't realize then that, in fact, the freedom I was seeking lay silent inside me all the time. With this knowledge, I took decisions in life which were independent and uniquely mine. Many looked flawed, wrong, hasty, risky, but I took them. They came from deep inside me, not from the surrounding competition and influences. The result is in front of me today, as I write this piece sitting in the comfort of my office in the middle of a busy working day.

Freedom is a state where one comes to realize one is unique, one of a kind on this Earth. Between idol adoration and idol copying, most of the time we miss this truthful realization. Charismatic and thought defining, Indian godman Rajneesh, known around the world as Osho, cited freedom as a need for everybody. He was precise when he said "freedom means that everybody is free to be unequal". He says further that "every individual is born with some specific talents, some specific genius to himself. That something in him needs to be discovered. Freedom can only bring out his talents, or else he will be equal to someone else. Osho said, "Equality and freedom cannot go together. They cannot coexist. If you choose equality, freedom has to be sacrificed. Genius is sacrificed, man's qualities are sacrificed. Everybody has to fit with the lowest and one denominator, only then you can be equal. Freedom gives you the power to be unequal. It opens the way to differ. It makes you what you are truly". [(7)]

To think one to be unequal is hardest when we live our lives by the measure of a yardstick. It is also the hardest state to achieve when one is a bundle of body and mind. Both shackle an individual. I ran to an idyllic location and took myself out from routine work on countless occasions to soak myself in freeness. But the body pinned me down on natural law and the mind ran on the created culture, holding me down. The body followed its urges and looked for satiation and I realized fleeing from the body was futile. In spite of this, ascetics try it all the time. They try to overcome the body rule by following a method of denial. They keep the body away from good food. They deprive the body of pleasure. They even try to inflict starvation, pain and torture. I see this spectacle even to this day when hundreds of "naked sadhus", Hindu puritans as they are known, visit holy sites across India during religious festivities. Various feats are claimed by each one of them. Some have lived buried under mud for years, others live standing, never rested lying down, and some have shunned food. These ascetics are revered by throngs of visitors for their power to beat the bodily urges as they continue to live. A phenomenal amount of denial is a way they believe they can get freedom from their body. I will never know definitively if they do achieve their freedom in this way.

I knew Buddha did the same many centuries ago and I scoured for his life teachings in my collected books. I found a book by Pankaj Mishra, *An End to Suffering*, in which he had written what I was looking for: "Yogic meditation having failed to bring insight, the Buddha decided to further limit his diet to soup or an occasional fruit. He further went naked, he refused to sit down, preferring to stand or squat on his heels. He went to sleep in a cemetery. By doing so, Buddha earned great respect from people around him, who, too, were on their path as wisdom seekers and had decided to follow Buddha in asceticism. They even asked him to 'announce the law' whenever he attained it." Mishra wrote further: "People were shocked one day when they saw Buddha eating porridge and a gruel. As the Buddha himself recalled, they had turned away in disgust, saying 'he is luxury-loving, he has forsaken his striving, he has become extravagant'. Buddha had then said, 'Though I have undergone severe ascetic practices, I cannot reach the special and wonderful knowledge and insight transcending the affairs of human beings. Could there be another way to attain enlightenment?' Buddha had given it up and gone back to taking care for his body."(8) Such denial of bodily needs will not help one realize spiritual goal. The body does not do any wrong. The body is a miracle where life plays its role. Nurturing a body is one's primary work.

The shackle a nurtured body throws upon an individual is its constant craving, which according to Buddha is the reason for all suffering. This very nature of suffering keeps one away from the path of seeking "good-life". Quoting teachings from Buddha, Pankaj Mishra writes: "Craving literally drives human beings. It is different from desire and in Buddha's teaching he does not seem to have disapproved of wanting per se. To want something out of one's free will, and with the right intention, is not craving. Craving came into being 'wherever that is which seems lovable and gratifying, there it comes into being and settles'. It made humans seek 'fresh pleasure now here and now there'. There is a craving to escape pain as well as for acquiring wealth, power, status, sensual pleasure as well as right opinions. This involves escape from here and now, to some place other, but to seek ceaselessly some new state of being while at the same time striving for permanence was to expose oneself to frustration."(9)

Buddha found that "those who are free from craving do not suffer". The wisdom to get away from craving is another way to freedom. I chose this path to earn my freedom. I chose it over other attractive options, such as riches, glamour or happiness. Each of these, I felt was measurable and thus quantifiable, so may start the cycle of craving inside me again for more. Nonetheless, the choice inside me for freedom must have a deep meaning somewhere. Why did it come spontaneously inside me? Why I did not take shelter in something else?

The famous Hindu-Bengali monk Narendranath Dutta, known more as Swami Vivekananda, came to my rescue as he had said it all in his teachings, 'The Evolution of Freedom'. "Freedom is the desire of human soul," he said.(10) He went further: "There was never a human race which did not worship God. Whether the God or Gods existed or not is not the question; but why this effort in trying to find or seek God? Because we remain in bondage, despite success and achievements. Nature and natural laws grind us down all the time, leaving us no option. It is everywhere. Thus, the human soul never forgets its freedom and is seeking it all the time. The search for freedom is the search that all religions take up; whether they know it or not, whether they can formulate it well or not, the idea is there. It is God which can give us the freedom. Freedom from natural laws. We have created God, Demon and Ghost, who subdue nature, for whom nature is not the almighty, for whom there is no law."

According to him, "the aim of human life is becoming free". All things in nature work as per law. "Everything that we perceive around us is struggling toward freedom. From the atom to the Man. From the insentient, lifeless particle of matter to the human soul. The whole universe is in fact the result of this struggle for freedom. Freedom from everything. The senses, whether of pleasure or pain. From good as well as evil. The idea of freedom is the only true idea of salvation."[11]

*

How to be free, remain free and still be a functional part of the social system was the next intriguing question I wanted to solve. I did not want to run away seeking freedom and be an outlaw. Freedom by way of freely sharing my abilities, skills, expertise and knowledge is a way I devised to seek freedom. Just like any energy-laden body in nature which works by dissipating its overload, humans, too, can follow this principle. In humans, this energy is knowledge, creativity, originality, resourcefulness, helpfulness, sacrifice, service, participation and more. It is a state of enablement, which could set one to freedom. Simple life tasks can set one to freedom, opening the shop in the middle of the night for a needy client sets one to freedom. Not doing them means you are holding on to something and are not free. Countless such daily actions were the way I found my freedom. It brings me to yet another passage from Eckhart Tolle where he says, "Non-resistance, non-judgement, and non-attachment are the three aspects of true freedom and enlightened living." He explains further: "These words do not mean that one should not enjoy good things in one's life, nor are they merely meant to provide some comfort in times of suffering. They in fact have a deeper purpose, to make one aware of the fleetingness of every situation, which is due to the transient nature of all forms, both good and bad."[12]

Tussle with God and Machine

Freedom is a powerful word and seeking it is everyone's eventual desire. While the body is bound by natural law, which it could not free from, it is the human mind which leads to freedom. As Zoe Cormier describes, "Our unrivaled mind may be what makes us human, but it is also what makes us profoundly miserable, anxious and confused." Cormier asks: "Does by thinking less do us good now and then and if so, what can help us think less?"(13)

Mind is an asset to humans. If humans are evolving, it is through thoughts and thinking. Then why think less? Why numb our senses when we have the power to control them and channel them? If the mind is dysfunctional at birth, it could be trained to be our liberator, too. We have created God out of our thoughts. God is where we seek our freedom. In God and in noble acts, we numb our wavering mind, cravings and channel our thoughts further. In godly acts, we control our mind and focus our thoughts. God is one who rolls out immense power, defines natural rules and laws, and can perform miracles. Taking shelter in God is to find freedom.

Unfortunately, God has lost its meaning in the modern world. People's faith in God is the lowest, if not lost. Not because God and expression of God is dead, but it suddenly looked powerless. We lacked proof of marvel and miracle. We want action to believe in his power, and God is not showing us a few, if not any. News of miracle healing, miracle sighting and miracle acts draws millions, and we turn toward starting to believe again. When the events turn out to be false, it makes us seek another answer. But faith in God has not diminished any. And we have come to accept he remains elusive for some reasons. Out of this vacuum has emerged artificial intelligence (AI). We have worked out another way, a more practical and modern version of God. It is this realization which made us create intelligent machines. In her book *Machines Who Think*, Pamela McCorduck quite rightly explains this whole effort as "an ancient wish of humans to forge the Gods".(14)

The start of modern artificial intelligence, in fact, originated from classical philosophers who attempted to describe the process of human thinking as the mechanical manipulation of symbols, and, therefore, the process of human thought could be mechanized. The modern-day computer is a culmination of this idea. The venture further inspired a handful of scientists to begin seriously discussing the possibility of building an electronic brain. This is a brain which performs supernatural tasks with the greatest conformity but without thinking.(15) In fact, we are in the process of creating thinking machines which are free from the mind. We have knowingly or unknowingly created them in pursuit of gaining freedom from thinking and wavering thoughts but still perform tasks. And tasks are what we love doing these days.

Since industrialization began, our culture has turned toward work. It has triggered rapid urbanization and a culture of performing tasks. This, in turn, fuels a need for everyone to work. We now work to live, and live to work. The world has suddenly turned to favor the best workers, the specialists. The "winner takes it all" effect seems to be the course for the future to evolve into and specialists are undoubtedly the winners. This sudden change allowed machines to come into work and outperform humans to take skills to ultimate perfection.

I vaguely remember a game of chess where IBM computer Deep Blue played Gary Kasparov, then the world champion. Deep Blue matched Kasparov move by move and was able to win one of the games. This experiment triggered insights into the working of the human mind. This was the start of a new way, where machines, too, started thinking. Since then, machines have performed an array of impressive feats, from flying planes, conducting surgeries, to composing music. Recently, the Saudi Arabian government granted citizenship for the first time to a machine, a robot named Sophia.(16)

*

We stood up and straightened our backs to evolve as humans from our chimpanzee ancestors to express freedom. We no longer climb the same tree and eat the same fruits but choose our own items from the *a la carte* menu. We remained social but expressed diversity because we have freedom. Freedom defines us and we pursued it to create AI, to express our free will. The power of choice between what to eat, where to travel next, what is the best buy and whom to connect with is slowly being determined by AI running in our smartphones. Yuval Harari thinks of the emergence of a new religion called "Dataism", where "the entire universe is perceived as a flow of data and organisms as biochemical algorithms".[(17)] Eventually, humans will be predictable and controllable beings. We will be naked as never before but this time the nudity is not physical, but biochemical. Work is underway to make this a reality soon. Countries are moving to collect biometric data of its citizens. Countries like India are spending billions of dollars in efforts to map their citizen. Basic services are only available when one is in the database, or they are denied. Complaints regarding functioning of biometric data because of age and physical changes, such as in case of an accident, are surfacing. I am sure soon chips will be inserted into bodies first as markers and later as processors that would monitor the being. In Harari's words, "Body implants will measure your heart rate, blood pressure, and brain activity 24 hours a day. Your smartphone will constantly analyze that data, and will, therefore, know your desires, likes and dislikes even better than you. We see versions of this today, with our Amazon accounts, which seem to know our taste in books and music better than we do. Humans will then stand hackable."[(18)]

Now I knew why I chose freedom over the rest of the things. With the chip inserted, I might walk past gates and doors, access lounges and lobbies, but when a clerk at the front desk of a hotel will greet me with my name right on arrival, I will realize my freedom is being infringed upon. We have chosen to be dependent on AI applications because it promise freedom, not to give away our true freedom. We enjoy the privacy of the smartphone when we make our choices to express freedom, not to pawn ourselves to an online vendor. The day we realize this, that we are being watched and influenced, be it by a smart software or anything else, we will start seeking our freedom from it. Freedom lays out more choices than any other entity, God or AI. The choice I will make with freedom will be my choices, out of my own intelligence. They will be chosen out of my conscience and alertness. With freedom, I may even opt out of the whole fiasco and invent another way of life.

In the End, it's all about a "Good Story"

Somehow, a small part in the book *The Big Picture* caught my attention. In it, author Sean Carroll wrote that "at the end of the day, or the end of your life, it does not matter so much that you were happy much of your time. Wouldn't you rather have a good story to tell?"(19) He had caught me in my thoughts dead right. We love stories and we come to live them. We love them and live them because they are playable, repeatable, comparable and shareable. We have turned to become nothing less than a bundle of stories.

Freedom helps us in crafting our own stories. This is where freedom plays its role. It helps us construct what we want to make and believe in. Failure to make such stories is the root of misery and unhappiness. And why not, it is the single greatest thing humans can leave behind. Stories are permanence, unlike many other things. Stories are defended and reaffirmed to last the longest. Stories connect individual lives, from their inner instincts to outer culture, ancient beliefs to modern discoveries, and more. Some to stand as inspiration and others as mere expression. Some to heal and others to pain. Some to be believed and others to be buried. Buddha and Jesus to us remain stories of sacrifices and selflessness. I am a Hindu not because I am any different from others, but just by the mythic stories which influenced me. A soldier jumps out of his sheltered trench uninstructed and charges at the enemy just because he has built a story. So do the rest of us, each time and every time. Thus, there exist stories of lives of countless men and women who walked the Earth. We decide to listen to some and connect, and to the others we remain unaware. Stories define what we are and stories will continue to emerge as long as humans exist.

In fact, it is through stories we have elevated ourselves to be humans. Yuval Harari describes this humorously, saying that "you can never convince a chimpanzee to give you a banana by promising him that after he dies, he will get limitless bananas in chimpanzee Heaven. Only Humans can believe such stories. This is why we rule the world, and chimpanzees are locked up in zoos and research laboratories". [(20)] He adds: "Stories have made us cooperate effectively with strangers because we believe in things like Gods, nations, money and human rights. Yet none of these things exists outside the stories that people invent and tell one another. There are no Gods in the universe, no nations, no money and no human rights, except in the common imagination of human beings."[(19)]

Stories make us what we are, and who we are. We never turn back on our stories. Our story is the final identity we leave behind. Do names, per se, like Charles Darwin, Steve Jobs, Barack Obama, Nelson Mandela, Gandhi, Michael Jackson, Dalai Lama, or Lady Diana give any hint of happiness, luxury, idealism, spiritualism, philanthropy, miracle healing? Surprisingly no – they are known only for their life stories. They have lived with freedom and expressed their will and desire to their best in the pursuit of freedom. In doing so, their life story put them on a pedestal as humans. This made me ponder: Does my tussle in life finally end with making a story? A story which would define my life, and more, make me feel good? A story connecting my culture, beliefs, upbringing, education, travels, struggles, confusions, achievements and, finally, my freedom? The story of my life when I am gone seemed a charming thought, but whether or not it was a worthy story of free will, remains my final tussle.

REFERENCES AND FURTHER READINGS:

Chapter 1

Welcome to life

1. Eckhart, T. (2005) A New Earth : Awakening of Your Life's Purpose. Pages 8-13.

2. Hee, K-H. and Kim, H-H. (1993) The Tears of My Soul: The True Story of a North Korean Spy.

3. Lunn, P. (2010) Basic Instincts :Human Nature and the New Economics. Pages 127-155.

4. Howard, B. (2013) Could Malcolm Gladwell's theory of cockpit culture apply to Asiana crash. https://news.nationalgeographic.com/news/2013/07/130709-asiana-flight-214-crash-korean-airlines-culture-outliers/ (Accessed March, 2019).

5. Carroll, S.M. (2017) The Big Picture: On the Origins of Life, Meaning, and the Universe Itself. Pages 119-122.

6. Eckhart T. (2001) The Power of Now: A Guide to Spiritual Enlightenment. Pages 89-106.

7. Kurzwell, R. (2005) The Singularity Is Near: When Humans Transcend Biology.

Chapter 2

Nature, Nurture and Fate

1. Kardener, S., Olofsson-Kardener, M. (2010) Breaking Free: How Chains From Childhood Keep Us From What We Want, Pages 1-20.

2. Dobelli, R. (2017) The Art of the Good Life. Pages 26-29.

3. Banerjee, B. (2000) Bengal is one of the poorest state in India. https://timesofindia.indiatimes.com/Bengal-one-

of-the-poorest-states-in-India/articleshow/17459558.cms. (Accessed, March 2019).

4. Harari, Y. N. (2017) Homo Deus: A Brief History of Tomorrow. Pages 49-56.

5. Kardener, S. Olofsson-Kardener, M. (2010) Breaking Free: How Chains From Childhood Keep Us From What We Want, Pages 1-20.

6. Galapagos Conservation Trust (2019) http://evolution.discoveringgalapagos.org.uk/evolution-zone/discovering-darwin/darwins-life/biography-early-life/. (Accessed, March 2019).

7. Sharma, M. D. (2016) Motivating Thoughts of Plato.

8. Leakey, R. and Lewin, R. (1977) Origins. Page 28.

9. Mishra P. (2004) An End to Suffering. Pages 153-173.

10. Dutt, I. A. (2018) How the Communists killed Bengal's Industry http://www.rediff.com/business/special/how-the-communists-killed-bengals-industry/20180319.htm. (Accessed March 2019)

11. Chakravarti, S. (2017) The Bengalis – A Portrait of a Community. Page 365.

12. Chakravarti, S. (2017) The Bengalis – A Portrait of a Community. Page 343.

Chapter 3

We are Product of Our Times

1. Dobelli, R. (2017) Art of the Good Life. Page 207.

2. National Geographic (2013). The 80s : The decade that made us. http://natgeotv.com/ca/the-80s-the-decade-that-made-us/about. (Accessed Jan 2019).

3. India Today (2018) Five ways how Rajiv Gandhi changed India forever https://www.indiatoday.in/india/story/5-ways-how-rajiv-gandhi-changed-india-forever-1318979-2018-08-20. (Accessed Jan 2019).

4. Cohen, R. (2017) Why Generation X Might Be Our Last Best Hope. https://www.vanityfair.com/style/2017/08/why-generation-x-might-be-our-last-best-hope. (Accessed Jan 2019).

5. Martin, A.S (2016) The Undetected Influence Of Generation X. https://www.forbes.com/sites/nextavenue/2016/09/13/the-undetected-influence-of-generation-x/#638ac6151efb. (Accessed Jan 2019).

6. Hoban, T. (2011) Steve Jobs would not have successed without supportive counterculture, https://socinnovation.wordpress.com/2011/11/11/steve-jobs-would-not-have-succeeded-without-supportive-counterculture/. (Accessed Jan 2019).

7. Brand, S. (1995) We owe it all to the Hippies, https://blog.kareldonk.com/wp-content/uploads/2015/05/we_owe_it_all_to_the_hippies.pdf. (Accessed March 2019).

8. Markoff, J (2005) What the Dormouse Said: How the Sixties Counterculture Shaped the Personal computer Industry. Pages 1-352.

9. Cadwalladr, C. (2013) Stewart Brand's Whole Earth Catalog, the book that changed the world, https://www.theguardian.com/books/2013/may/05/stewart-brand-whole-earth-catalog. (Accessed Jan 2019).

Chapter 4

Origin of Tussle

1. Eckhart, T. (2005) A New Earth : Awakening of Your Life's Purpose. Pages 93-94.

2. Christenfeld, N. and Hill, E. (1995) Whose baby are you? Nature 378: 669.

3. A failure to replicate Christenfeld & Hill (1995), https://www.researchgate.net/publication/2242586_Do_Babies_Resemble_Their_Fathers_More_Than_Their_Mothers_A_Failure_to_Replicate_Christenfeld_and_Hill_1995, (Accessed Jan 2019).

4. Pittman, F. (1994) Man Enough: Fathers, Sons, and the Search for Masculinity. Pages 1-336.

5. Friedman, T. L. and Mandelbaum, M. (2011). That Used to be US. Pages 59-65.

Chapter 5

Midlife Midley

1. Kardener, S., Kardener, M. O. (2010) Breaking Free: How Chains From Childhood Keep Us From What We Want. Pages 135-137.

2. Olster, S. (2010) Warren Buffet's wisdom for powerful women. http://fortune.com/2010/10/06/warren-buffetts-wisdom-for-powerful-women/. (Accessed Jan 2019).

3. Singh, K. (2002) Truth, Love and Little Malice. Pages 401-402.

Chapter 6

Searching for Identity

1. Radford, T. (2011) Untold Story of Human Evolution. https://www.theguardian.com/science/2011/apr/25/evolution-human-history-apes. (Accesssed March 2019).

2. Leakey, R. and Lewin, R. (1977) Origin. Page 31.

3. Marks, J. (2009) The Nature of Humanness. In: The Oxford Handbook of Archaelogy. Pages 237-253.

4. Goodman, A., Heath, D., and Lindee, M . S. (2003). Genetic Nature/Culture: Anthropology and Science Beyond the Two Culture Divide. Berkeley: University of California Press.

5. Singh , D.(1993). Body shape and women's attractiveness: the critical role of waist-to-hip ratio. Human Nature. Pages 297-321.

6. Yu, D. and Shepargd, H. (1998). Is beauty in the eye of the beholder? Nature, 326: Pages 391-392.

7. Wood,W., and Eaglya, H. (2002).A cross-cultural analysis of the behavior ofwomen and men: implications for the origins of sex differences. Psychological Bulletin, 128: Pages 699-727.

8. Singh, K. (2014), Agnostic Khushwant There is no God. Page 106.

9. Yuko, El. (2017) American Cult: 5 Spiritual Groups That Went Too Far, https://www.rollingstone.com/culture/culture-lists/american-cult-5-spiritual-groups-that-went-too-far-202224/the-peoples-temple-1955-1978-202246/. (Accessed March 2019).

10. Harari, Y. N. (2016) Homo Deus: A Brief History of Tomorrow. Page 299.

11. Wilson, E, O. (2012) The Social Conquest of Earth. Pages 109-119.

12. Angier, N. (2012) Edward O. Wilson's New Take on Human Nature. https://www.smithsonianmag.com/science-nature/edward-o-wilsons-new-take-on-human-nature-160810520/. (Accessed March 2019).

Chapter 7

Answers in Culture

1. Bhanji, J. P. and Delgado, M. R. (2014) The Social Brain and Reward: Social Information Processing in the Human Striatum, https://www.ncbi.nlm.nih.gov/pmc/articles/PMC3890330/ (Accessed, March 2019).
2. Bhagavad Gita (2018) https://vaniquotes.org/wiki/Fruitive_activities_(Bhagavad-gita). (Accessed March 2019).
3. Marks, J. (2009) The Nature of Humanness. In: The Oxford Handbook of Archaelogy. Pages 237-253.
4. Wikipedia (2019) List of Invasions, https://en.wikipedia.org/wiki/List_of_invasions. (Accessed March 2019).
5. Sengupta, H. (2015) Being Hindu : Old Faith, New World and You. Pages 90-95.
6. Sengupta, H. (2015) Being Hindu : Old Faith, New World and You. Page 86.
7. Mark, J. (2012) Ancient India, https://www.ancient.eu/india/. (Accessed March 2019).
8. Nathwani, P. (2016) Here's what make Indian constitution unique, http://www.parimalnathwani.com/heres-what-makes-the-indian-constitution-unique/. (Accessed March 2019).
9. Sengupta, H. (2015) Being Hindu : Old Faith, New World and You. Page 95.
10. Ricci, K. (2019) Hinduism and Democracy: The Transition of India to Democracy and its Implications for Islam. https://freshwriting.nd.edu/volumes/2014/essays/hinduism-and-democracy-the-transition-of-india-to-democracy-and-its-implications-for-islam (Accessed March 2019).

11. Sengupta, H. (2015) Being Hindu : Old Faith, New World and You. Page 58.

12. Sengupta, H. (2015) Being Hindu : Old Faith, New World and You. Page 5.

13. Chellappan, K. (2011) New research debunks aryan invasion theory. American Journal of Human Genetics. Also https://www.dnaindia.com/india/report-new-research-debunks-aryan-invasion-theory-1623744 (Accessed March 2019).

14. Flisar, E. (2018) Seeking spirituality and an Indian visa. http://www.thehindu.com/life-and-style/travel/evald-flisar-on-his-arduous-journey-from-slovenia-to-india/article23902240.ece?homepage=true (Accessed January 2019).

15. Chakravarti, S. The Bengalis – A Portrait of a Community. Pages xvi-xxxv.

16. Krishna Kumar, V. (2018) A Legendary Creative Math Genius: Srinivasa Ramanujan. https://www.psychologytoday.com/au/blog/psychology-masala/201802/legendary-creative-math-genius-srinivasa-ramanujan. (Accessed January 2019).

Chapter 8

Taming Mind

1. Wheeler, P. E. (1984) The evolution of bipedality and loss of functional body hair in hominids, Journal of Human Evolution. Volume 13. Pages 91-98.

2. Hendrickson, J. (2012) Why is it impossible to stop thinking, to render the mind a complete blank? https://www.scientificamerican.com/article/ask-the-brains-why-impossible-to-stop-thinking/. (Accessed March 2019).

3. Yuval, N. H. (2016) Home Deus – A Brief history of Tomorrow. Page 49.

4. Bhagavad Gita, https://www.holy-bhagavad-gita.org/chapter/5/verse/22. (Accessed March 2019).

5. Jill, J. (2013) Pleasures of good life, https://fellowsjill.wordpress.com/2013/09/20/pleasure-and-the-good-life/. (Accessed March 2019).

6. Bentham, J. (1988) The Principles of Morals and Legislation. Pages 1-352.

7. Sharot, T. et al (2009) Dopamine Enhances Expectation of Pleasure in Humans Curr Biol, 19. Pages 2077–2080. https://www.ncbi.nlm.nih.gov/pmc/articles/PMC2801060/ (Accessed March 2019).

8. White, M. P. and Dolan, P. (2009) Accounting for the Richness of Daily Activities. http://pauldolan.co.uk/wp-content/uploads/2011/07/Accounting-for-the-rishness-of-daily-activities.pdf. (Accessed 2019).

9. Tolle, E. (2005), A New Earth – Awakening to your Life's Purpose. Page 124.

10. Maguire, E. A., Woollett, K. and Spiers, H.J. (2006) London Taxi Drivers and Bus Drivers: A Structural MRI and Neuropsychological. Hippocampus 16. Pages

1091–1101. https://www.fil.ion.ucl.ac.uk/Maguire/Maguire2006.pdf. (Accessed March 2019).

11. Bartels, L. (2008) Neuroplasticity and the Brain That Changes Itself. https://sharpbrains.com/blog/2008/11/12/neuroplasticity-and-the-brain-that-changes-itself/. (Accessed March 2019).

12. Wikipedia. https://en.wikipedia.org/wiki/Hebbian_theory (Accessed March 2019).

13. Gaser, C., and Schlaug, G.(2013) Brain structures differ between musicians and non-musicians. https://www.ncbi.nlm.nih.gov/pubmed/14534258. (Accessed March 2019).

14. Davidson, R. J. and Lutz, A. (2007) Buddha's Brain: Neuroplasticity and Meditation. https://centerhealthyminds.org/assets/files-publications/DavidsonBuddhaIEEESignalProcessingMagazine.pdf. (Accessed March 2019).

Chapter 9

Mastery of Body

1. Tolle, E. (2005) The New Earth – Awakening of Your Life's Purpose. Page 132.

2. Buravisit, O. (1989) Family Sex Composition Preferences and Contraceptive Use in Thailand : A Relative Risk Analysis. Journal of Population and Social Studies, Volume 2. Pages 100-114. Also http://repository.li.mahidol.ac.th/dspace/bitstream/123456789/3274/1/pr-ar-orapen-1989.pdf. Accessed March 2019).

3. Tolle, E. (2005) The New Earth – Awakening of Your Life's Purpose. Page 49.

4. Baumeister, R. F. and Bushman, B.J. (2016) Social Psychology and Human Nature. Chapter 3: The Self. Pages 71-117.

5. Tolle, E. (2005) The New Earth – Awakening of Your Life's Purpose. Pages 148-151.

6. Cormier, Z. (2013) Gene switches make prairie voles fall in love. Nature News. http://www.nature.com/news/gene-switches-make-prairie-voles-fall-in-love-1.13112. (Accessed, 2019).

7. Wikipidia, (2019) https://en.wikipedia.org/wiki/Monogamy_in_animals. (Accessed March 2019).

8. Blasio, B. de. and Menin, J. (2015). From Cradle to Cane: The Cost of Being a Female Consumer A Study of Gender Pricing in New York City. https://www1.nyc.gov/assets/dca/downloads/pdf/partners/Study-of-Gender-Pricing-in-NYC.pdf. (Accessed, March 2019).

9. Saini, A. (2017) Inferior: How Science Got Women Wrong. Pages 1-224.

10. Saini, A. (2017) Inferior: How Science Got Women Wrong. Pages 42-45.

11. Zihlman, A. (1983) Chapter 5 : Women the Gatherer. In : Archaeology, edited by Kelley Hays-Gilpin, David S. Whitley. Pages 91-105.

12. Booth, H. (2017) Kingdom of Women: The Society Where Man is Never the Boss. https://www.theguardian.com/lifeandstyle/2017/apr/01/the-kingdom-of-women-the-tibetan-tribe-where-a-man-is-never-the-boss. (Accessed March 2019).

13. Buckner, W. (2017) Romantizing the hunter-gatherer https://quillette.com/2017/12/16/romanticizing-hunter-gatherer/. (Accessed March 2019).

14. Cobb, M. (2015) Sexism in science: did Watson and Crick really steal Rosalind Franklin's data? https://www.theguardian.com/science/2015/jun/23/sexism-in-science-did-watson-and-crick-really-steal-rosalind-franklins-data. (Accessed March 2019).

15. Saini, A. (2017) Inferior: How Science Got Women Wrong. Page 5.

16. Leakey, R. and Lewin, R. (1977) Origins. Page 237.

17. Saini, A. (2017) Inferior: How Science Got Women Wrong. Page 234.

18. Wikipidia (2019) https://en.wikipedia.org/wiki/Ardhanarishvara. (Accessed March 2019).

19. Woddy Allen's Great Quotes, https://exploringyourmind.com/woody-allen-great-quotes/. (Accessed March 2019).

20. Boorstein, M. and Gately, G. (2018) More than 300 priests listed in Pennsylvania report on catholic church sex abuse. https://www.washingtonpost.com/news/acts-of-faith/wp/2018/08/14/pennsylvania-grand-jury-report-on-sex-abuse-in-catholic-church-will-list-hundreds-of-accused-predator-priests/?utm_term=.224393e473f6. (Accessed, March 2019).

21. Harari, Y. H. (2016) Homo Deus: The Brief History of Tomorrow. Page 137.

22. Morris, D. (1969) The Human Zoo. Page 72.

23. Ram Das (2004) Paths to God – Living the Bhagavad Gita. Pages 127-158.

24. Hindustan times (2018) Doctor pushes wife off hilltop in Nepal, updates Facebook page for 6 months: Cops. https://www.hindustantimes.com/india-news/gorakhpur-doctor-kills-ex-wife-keeps-her-social-media-accounts-running-to-deceive-family/story-l6pE7bfeIyUJYu5EOfX10I.html. (Accessed March 2019).

25. Wikipedia (2019) Gobekli Tepe. https://en.wikipedia.org/wiki/G%C3%B6bekli_Tepe. (Accessed March 2019).

Chapter 10

Choose Purpose over Happiness

1. Dobelli, R. (2017) The Art of the Good Life. Page ix.

2. Haig, M. (2015) Reasons to Stay Alive. Page 56.

3. Haig, M. (2015) Reasons to Stay Alive. Page 165.

4. Haig, M. (2015) Reasons to Stay Alive. Page 189.

5. Harari, Y. N. (2011) Sapiens : A Brief History of Humankind. Page 425.

6. Kingsley, P. (2018) It's Cold, Dark and Lacks Parking. But Is This Finnish Town the World's Happiest? https://www.nytimes.com/2018/12/24/world/europe/finland-happiness-social-services.html. (Accessed March 2019).

7. Buettner, D.(2017) Blue Zones of Happiness. https://www.nationalgeographic.com/magazine/2017/11/worlds-happiest-places/. (Accessed March 2019).

8. Helliwell, J., Layard, R. and Sachsat, J. (2017) World Happiness Report. https://s3.amazonaws.com/happiness-report/2018/WHR_web.pdf. (Accessed March 2019).

9. Friedman, T.L. and Mandelbaum, M. (2011) That Used to be Us: How America Fell Behind in the World It Invented and How We Can Come Back. Pages 271-275.

10. Wikipidia (2019) Where to invade next. https://en.wikipedia.org/wiki/Where_to_Invade_Next.

11. World Happiness Report 2017 (2017) http://worldhappiness.report/ed/2017/

12. Tolle, E. (2006) The power of Now, A New Earth : Awakening of your life"s Purpose. Pages 157-160.

13. Hariri, Y. N. (2016). Homo Dues A Brief Hostory of Tomorrow. Page 38.

14. World Happiest Report 2017 (2017) http://worldhappiness.report/ed/2017/. (Accessed March 2019).

15. Patanaik, D. (2009) East Vs West : The Myths that Mystify, https://www.ted.com/talks/devdutt_pattanaik?language=en. (Accessed March 2019).

16. Dobelli, R. (2017) The Art of the Good Life. Pages ix–53.

17. Hariri, Y. N. (2016). Homo Dues A Brief Hostory of Tomorrow. Page 37.

18. Baumeister, R. F. and Bushman, B. (2008) Social Psychology and Human Nature: Brief Version. Pages 69-114.

19. Nyaribari, L. (2010) Soverignty of the Mind

20. Hariri, Y. N. (2016). Homo Dues A Brief History of Tomorrow. Pages 1-82.

21. Ng, Y-K. and Ng, S. (2019) Road to Happiness. https://www.utilitarianism.com/prof-ng/ (Accessed march 2019).

22. MacAndrew, F. T. (2016) Don't try to be happy. We're programmed to be dissatisfied. https://www.theguardian.com/commentisfree/2016/aug/17/psychology-happiness-contentment-humans-aspire-goals-accomplish-evolution. (Accessed March 2019).

23. Smith, T. W., Son, J. and Schapiro, B. (2015) Trends in Psychological Well-Being, 1972-2014. http://www.norc.org/PDFs/GSS%20Reports/GSS_PsyWellBeing15_final_formatted.pdf. (Accessed March 2019).

24. Allen, W.C. (2017) This Endless Moment. Page 44.

25. Lyubomirsky, S.; Sheldon, K. M. and Schkade, D. (2005) Pursuing Happiness: The Architecture of Sustainable Change, Review of General Psychology, Vol. 9, No. 2, 111–131.

26. Wikipidia (2019) Amish. https://en.wikipedia.org/wiki/Amish. (Accessed March 2019).

27. Miller, S. B. (2016) More Than Happy: The Wisdom of Amish Parenting. Pages 1-336.

Chapter 11

Ending of Tussle

1. Dobelli, R. (2017) The Art of the good life, pp ix in foreword.

2. Morris, D. (1970) The Naked Ape. Page 9.

3. Morris, D. (1994) The Human Zoo. Page 1-162.

4. Harari, Y. N. (2011) Sapiens – A brief History of Humankind. Page 389.

5. Tolle, E. (2006) The Power of Now, A New Earth – Awakening of your life"s Purpose. Pages 129-163.

6. Branson, B. (2008) Business Stripped Bare : Adventures of a Global Entreprenuer. Page 7.

7. Osho (2012) Talks on the Isha Upanishad : I am That. Page 236.

8. Mishra, P. (2004) An end to suffering : The Buddha in the World. Pages 153-173

9. Mishra, P. (2004) An End to Suffering : The Buddha in the world. Pages 187-213.

10. The Complete Works of Swami Vivekananda/ Volume 1/Karma-Yoga/Freedom (2019). http://swamivivekanandaquotesgarden.blogspot.com/2013/04/

swami-vivekananda-quotes-on-freedom.html. (Accessed March 2019).

11. The Complete Works of Swami Vivekananda/ Volume 1/Karma-Yoga/Freedom (2019). http:// swamivivekanandaquotesgarden.blogspot.com/2013/04/ swami-vivekananda-quotes-on-freedom.html (Accessed March 2019).

12. Eckhart, T. (2005) A New Earth : Awakening of Your Life's Purpose.

13. Cormier, Z. (2015) Sex, Drugs, and Rock 'n' Roll: The Science of Hedonism and the Hedonism of Science. Introdution.

14. MaCorduck, P. (2004) Machine who Thinks. Pages 381-416.

15. History of Artificial Intelligence (2019) https:// en.wikipedia.org/wiki/History_of_artificial_intelligence. (Accessed March 2019).

16. Wikipidia (2019) https://en.wikipedia.org/wiki/Sophia_ (robot). (Accessed March 2019).

17. Hariri, Y. N. (2016). Homo Dues A Brief Hostory of Tomorrow. Pages 428-462.

18. Harari, Y. N. The Myth of Freedom (2019) https://www. theguardian.com/books/2018/sep/14/yuval-noah-harari-the-new-threat-to-liberal-democracy. (Accessed March 2019).

19. Carroll, S. (2017) The Big Picture – On the Origins of Life, Meaning and the Universe Itself. Page 426.

20. Harari, Y. N. (2017) The Power of Imagination. https:// www.ynharari.com/topic/power-and-imagination/. (Accessed March 2019).

About the Author

Partho Dhang earned a Ph.D. from the University of Madras in India. He is a zoologist, consultant, author and entrepreneur. He is a prolific writer in the scientific world and also a regular speaker in international conferences around the world. He has published over 50 peer-reviewed papers in international journals of repute, in addition to four scientific books with a prestigious UK-based publishing house. He also serves as a panelist and adjudicator for the award of the degree of doctorate for a number of universities and has evaluated more than 25 doctoral theses.

Lately, he has added business training to his expertise portfolio, providing consultancy to people in the service industry for start-ups as well as self-improvement. Extensively travelled on business and self-exploration, he has keen interest in history, people, culture and environment.

Currently, he lives in the Philippines and India.